BRIGITTE
SCHMIDT

THE HARBRACE CASEBOOKS IN POLITICAL SCIENCE
Under the General Editorship of
A L A N F. W E S T I N , *Columbia University*

The Uses of Power (1962)
The Third Branch of Government (1963)
The Centers of Power (1964)

The Centers of Power

3 Cases in American National Government

CONTRIBUTORS

Louis W. Koenig
NEW YORK UNIVERSITY

Hugh Douglas Price
SYRACUSE UNIVERSITY

Alan F. Westin
COLUMBIA UNIVERSITY

A HARBRACE CASEBOOK IN POLITICAL SCIENCE

The Centers of Power

3 Cases in American National Government

EDITED BY

Alan F. Westin COLUMBIA UNIVERSITY

NEW YORK · CHICAGO · BURLINGAME

Harcourt, Brace & World, Inc.

CONTENTS

INTRODUCTION

COURSES in American government or introduction to government usually range over the spectrum of political power, exploring which uses of power are deemed legitimate and which are not. Through commentary and examples drawn from American national experience, the student learns what a shifting and dynamic boundary there is between legitimacy and illegitimacy, and how the study of power as a motive force in human and political affairs is one of the most fascinating, complex, and important inquiries for both the scholar and the political activist.

In the parent volume to this book (*The Uses of Power,* published in 1962), we presented seven documentary depth studies covering each of the major arenas of political power within the American system of government. These cases covered the Presidency, Congress, the state and federal courts, the regulatory agencies, the party system, state and local government, and pressure groups. The large number of adoptions that book is enjoying and the flurry of pleased comments it attracted from instructors convinced us that the reconstruction of leading incidents in depth, with accompanying commentary and analysis, is an ideal way to test the assumptions of political science about how government and politics really function in America.

However, it soon became clear that many courses in American government and introduction to government just did not have the time to tackle seven case studies. Many suggestions were made to us that a few case studies focusing specifically on the national centers of power in order to illuminate a wide range of political problems would be warmly appreciated in such courses.

We offer here our response to those requests: three episodes that have as their sites the three national centers of power—the Presidency, Congress, and the Supreme Court. Each of these three cases has been written (or reworked) for this volume to touch on many of the problems that are more fully explored in *The Uses of Power.*

The first of these case studies is President Kennedy's intervention in the steel-pricing crisis of 1962 and its impact on the Presidency. In it, the story of the business collision with the Chief Executive, with its resulting shock waves, unfolds. The case assesses both the immediate setting of 1962 and the crucial aftermath developments of 1963. The second case study describes the Congressional rejection of the Kennedy aid-to-education bills of 1961–

64. It delves into the labyrinth of Congressional machinery, explaining step by step how the legislative process responded to unusual pressures from citizens and interest groups. The last case details the story of the Supreme Court's reaction to state-police wiretapping and eavesdropping practices down to 1964, showing how constitutional doctrine is affected by technological advances and how federal and state courts view their respective roles of punishing lawbreakers while protecting individual civil liberties.

Throughout these case studies, readers will find a focus that includes both men and institutions, ideals and self-interest, groups and "forces." For us, a focus on anything less than these cannot convey the realities of government. We hope, therefore, that these three "all-purpose" cases will enliven and enrich student encounters with the subtle blend of power and purpose that makes up politics in the United States.

ALAN F. WESTIN

1

THE PRESIDENCY

Kennedy and Steel

The Great Price Dispute

Louis W. Koenig

PRESIDENTIAL power is largely an abstraction that is only partially visible in the day-to-day business of government. It takes a time of crisis to reveal the dimensions of the office of President of the United States in specific and concrete ways. The resources at the President's disposal are perhaps not wholly clear even to the Chief Executive himself until crisis galvanizes members of his personal staff and sends them scurrying to ready the weapons of administrative power.

The President's personal style of action is of key importance in defining the limits of power. If the President is of passive inclination, he may do little or nothing when faced with crisis. He may simply take refuge in drift and delay. If he is more activist by nature, however, he can substantially alter the course of events. He can deploy his subordinates, rally public opinion, activate other branches of government, and thereby achieve his purposes.

This case examines President John F. Kennedy's response to a grave crisis of Presidential prestige and business confidence during his second year of office.

JOHN F. KENNEDY'S capacity for initiative had been well tested in his political career before his assumption of the Presidency, culminating in an extraordinary drive for the Democratic nomination and a whirlwind campaign that found him crossing and recrossing the country. His goals were conveyed by the phrase "The New Frontier," and his means for reaching those goals were "to get the country moving again." He felt that the President should take a positive, active position of leadership toward increasing productivity, checking inflation, reducing unemployment, stepping up economic growth, and improving American industry's ability to compete in international markets.

The new President's first White House Message to Congress (in February 1961) laid the groundwork for implementing these broad goals. He presented detailed recommendations on improving the national balance of payments. "We must place maximum emphasis on expanding our exports," the Message said. "Our costs and prices must therefore be kept low; and the government must play a more vigorous part in helping to enlarge foreign markets for American goods and services." But he noted that

> export promotion efforts, no matter how well devised or energetically pursued, will not be effective unless American goods are competitively priced. Our domestic policies—of government, of business, and of labor—must be directed to maintaining competitive costs, improving productivity, and stabilizing or where possible lowering prices.

The President set up an Advisory Committee on Labor and Management Policy to "encourage productivity gains, advance automation, and encourage sound wage policies and price stability." The Committee proved its worth to the Administration during the March-April negotiations between the United Steelworkers of America and the steel companies, when it helped to negotiate a new labor contract signed on April 6, 1962. The new contract provided only modest increases in wages and benefits—well within projected productivity gains and therefore noninflationary according to Presidential economic advisors. The President felt particular satisfaction that this settlement had departed from past steel negotiations. Unlike earlier settlements, this new contract could not be blamed for setting off a new inflationary spiral. The President could therefore contemplate the pact as a further assurance that American prices would remain competitive in the world market. He and his Administration thus had a sense of well-being following the end of steel wage negotiations.

A few days had to elapse before all signatories to the new pact set their official seals of approval on it. The week ended with peace practically assured in the steel industry but with ratification a few days away. The week of April 9 began placidly as the final signatures went on the necessary documents and the settlement became official. No longer did the dreary memory of the 116-day strike of 1959–60 hang like a storm cloud over the industry; no longer did inevitable crisis loom ahead.

Tuesday, April 10

A Shattered Calm

Tuesday afternoon, April 10, was one of those rare interludes at the White House in which major trouble spots were momentarily dormant. For an hour or so, the burdens of state seemed less oppressive than usual. As events on that afternoon were later reconstructed by the New York *Times,* the President called his personal secretary, Mrs. Evelyn Lincoln, to check the remainder of the day's agenda.

"You have Mr. Blough at a quarter to six," said Mrs. Lincoln. No stranger in the White House, Roger M. Blough was chairman of the board of the United States Steel Corporation, the nation's third biggest enterprise in assets and its largest producer of steel.

"Mr. Blough?" the President exclaimed.

"Yes."

Surely there must be a mistake, thought the President. Perhaps he had better check with his Appointments Secretary. "Get me Kenny O'Donnell," he said.

There was no mistake. According to O'Donnell, Blough was definitely scheduled for 5:45.

This appointment had been made necessary by a meeting that afternoon in the board room of U.S. Steel on the twentieth floor of 71 Broadway in lower Manhattan. Nine of the corporation's twelve-member executive committee, including Leslie B. Worthington, president, and Robert C. Tyson, chairman of the finance committee, were present. Roger Blough, a soft-spoken fifty-eight-year-old man, presided. To his duties as board chairman, for which he is paid $283,333 annually, Blough brings a legal background, a nimble, well-organized mind, and the tenacity of those bygone square-jawed iron and steel magnates whose portraits adorn the walls of Union Clubs in many an industrial city.

For several months before this meeting in the board room, U.S. Steel officials had been hinting in public speeches and company reports that steel prices would have to rise to meet increasing costs. In a widely publicized lecture, for example, on March 14 at the Tenth Annual Management Conference at the University of Chicago, Worthington had complained of the "squeeze" of rising costs on profits and had all but said that a price increase was necessary.

Strangely, U.S. Steel had given no hints of a price rise in numerous direct contacts with Kennedy Administration officials. Thus no price boost was expected in the April contract that was to become effective on July 1, 1962. But U.S. Steel's executive committee was gathered to do what the Kennedy Administration neither wanted nor expected it to do. The sales department, Blough was disclosing, had concurred in a recommendation to raise prices by 3.5 per cent. This would add about $6 to the going average of $170 a ton. Blough had checked with the public relations department, and it reported what everyone knew: a price increase would be unpopular. The executive committee nevertheless voted unanimously to go ahead.

With the decision made, Blough enplaned for Washington, while word was telephoned ahead to the White House that he wished to discuss something "important" about steel with the President. The President had since the outset of his Administration been earnestly trying to assure the business and financial communities of his friendly attitude toward their legitimate aspirations and activities. The appointments to leading economic posts in his Administration were carefully in keeping with this purpose. Secretary of Commerce Luther H. Hodges had left a distinguished career in business. Secretary of the Treasury Douglas Dillon, a Republican and former official of the Eisenhower Administration, hailed from a prominent New York investment house. Secretary of Defense Robert N. McNamara, also a Republican, had come from the Ford Motor Company. Many officials at the secondary levels of these departments had also made their mark in the business world.

In contrast to the Truman Administration, the leading members of the Kennedy Administration dealing with economic policy were moderates. In speeches and actions, the Kennedy Administration had sought to demonstrate a sympathetic understanding of business problems. The approach had earned the Administration a good business press, although it did not allay widespread business suspicion that the Administration was basically pro-labor and anti-business and would manifest its partiality in time.

Shortly after 5:45 Blough handed the President a four-page mimeographed press release about to be sent to newspapers in Pittsburgh and New York. "Pittsburgh, Pa., April 10—," the release read, "For the first time in nearly four years, United States Steel today announced an increase in the general level of its steel prices."

The President rushed through the announcement and immediately summoned Arthur J. Goldberg, the Secretary of Labor. The Secretary, who had watched over the negotiation of the new wage contract for steelworkers, had assured the President that its minimal benefits for labor, which the Administration, by considerable persuasion, had induced the Steelworkers union to accept, were not substantial enough to necessitate a price rise.

Within minutes, Goldberg traveled the four blocks from the Labor Department to the President's office.

Grimly, Kennedy gave Goldberg the U.S. Steel press release, remarking that it had already been distributed to the newspapers. Goldberg glanced over it and asked Blough what the point of the meeting was since the price decision had already been made.

Blough said he thought it a matter of courtesy to inform the President personally. It was hardly a courtesy, Goldberg retorted, to announce a decision and confront the President with an accomplished fact.

A half-hour discussion ensued, in which the President kept his temper, while Goldberg turned on Blough with some heat. The price increase, the Secretary declared, would imperil the government's entire economic policy, damage the interests of U.S. Steel, and undercut responsible collective bargaining. Finally, and climactically, Goldberg said, the price decision could be viewed only as a double-cross of the President of the United States because during the contract negotiations the company had not given the Administration the slightest hint of its intention to raise prices.

Despite the mounting acerbity, Blough defended his company's position in a quiet voice and then departed.

President Kennedy now considered which members of his Administration might join his discussion with Secretary Goldberg. Presumably, in this difficult hour, he wished to have at hand colleagues who were knowledgeable in the technical economics of the steel situation and others who could help assess his own administrative and political needs. The latter would be affected by any action he might decide to take on the steel question. In looking about for staff people to summon, Kennedy had a wide choice. He could turn to the Treasury, Commerce, and Justice Departments. Likewise, he could dip into several agencies situated close to his own office. Closest of all is the White House Staff, including the President's Special Counsel, Press Secretary, Appointments Secretary, Assistant for Congressional Relations, several administrative assistants, a scientific adviser, the Assistant for National Security Affairs, and sundry other assistants. The White House Staff is smaller and less formally organized under Kennedy than it was under Eisenhower to facilitate Kennedy's control and personal use of the staff.

The men who fill the White House Staff positions reflect Kennedy's Presidential style and, in a sense, his own personal and political history. A typical member of the group that formed around Kennedy prior to his election to the Senate in 1952 is Kenneth ("Kenny") O'Donnell, a tough, rather dour ex-football captain and Harvard roommate of brother Robert ("Bobby") Kennedy. O'Donnell is the President's Appointments Secretary, a master arranger and implementer who sees that the right people show up at the right time and that things happen when they should. This group is composed of the political technicians; large ideas and high policy are seldom their concern. The latter is the province of Kennedy's "Eggheads"—several *émigré* faculty members from Harvard and M.I.T., of whom McGeorge Bundy, Special Assistant for National Security Affairs and a former Harvard dean, is representative.

A link between the two groups is the President's Special Counsel, Theodore Sorensen, a Nebraskan whose remarkable knack for reproducing Kennedy's verbal style has long established him as Kennedy's chief speechwriter. Sorensen is more than a ghost, however. As Kennedy said, "All domestic matters go through him." Another link between the two groups is the Attorney General, the President's brother Robert. In matters both of high policy and of political management, Robert is the President's closest confidant.

Beyond the White House Staff, Kennedy could obtain succor from several units of the Executive Office of the President—the Bureau of the Budget, the National Security Council, and the Council of Economic Advisers. The latter agency prepares the President's Economic Report to Congress each January and conducts special studies to recommend policies to the President that will foster the economy's highest productivity and maximum employment levels.

President Kennedy had now decided which of his colleagues to summon: the three members of the Council of Economic Advisers. The chairman, lean and scholarly looking Walter W. Heller, a University of Minnesota economist, came hastily from his office; Kermit Gordon of Williams College, a second member, followed in three minutes; the third member, James Tobin, also an economist, hurried back to his own office later that evening.

While the CEA members were arriving, several White House Staff officials augmented the growing circle in the President's office. Sorensen came in, followed by O'Donnell and Andrew Hatcher, Acting Press Secretary for Pierre Salinger, who was on vacation.

With the White House aides, CEA officials, and Secretary Goldberg assembled, the President, for the first time since the crisis had exploded, really let himself go. Normally, he holds himself under the close rein of Harvardian moderation, but now his temper flared. He had been double-crossed, he said, deliberately double-crossed. The office of the President had been affronted. The national interest had been flouted. Bitterly he recalled, "My father always told me that all businessmen were sons-of-bitches but I never believed it till now."

Introducing United States Steel

The object of the President's wrath, the United States Steel Corporation, was an industrial colossus, a complex of steel-making facilities, ore and coal enterprises, railroads, ships, and a cement company. Although there were many other giants in the American steel industry, U.S. Steel enjoyed distinction as the only nationwide producer of steel. Other major steel-producers had their basic facilities in one or two main areas, such as the East or the Midwest. The second largest steel enterprise, the Bethlehem Steel Corporation, had facilities on the East and West coasts,* but only U.S. Steel was truly national at that time. It had major facilities from Fairless Works at Morrisville, Pennsylvania, through the Pittsburgh-Youngstown and Chicago areas, through Birmingham in the South, to Geneva, Utah, and Pittsburg and Torrance, California, in the West. Furthermore, most of the other steel companies had more limited product lines than did U.S. Steel.

U.S. Steel's creation in 1901 was a signal event, the climax of a profound economic movement, under way for a generation, that concentrated industry and transportation in huge units. Like other concentrations of its type, U.S. Steel tended to reduce competition and facilitate economies in manufacture, transportation, marketing, administration, and finance. In the 1920's, U.S. Steel was judged a "good" trust while comparable empires like the Standard Oil Corporation were broken up. In the New Deal era, U.S. Steel's capitulation to the CIO's demand for collective-bargaining recognition was a historic development. New Deal analysts portrayed the company as an economic behemoth asserting "price leadership"—in effect setting prices that other steel-producers faithfully followed.

The 1950's witnessed a considerable slippage in the relative strength of U.S. Steel in the industry. Its share of the market fell from 30.1 per cent of the industry total in 1955 to 25.4 per cent in 1961. From a high of 85 million tons shipped in 1955, U.S. Steel's volume of tons shipped fell to 60 million in 1958, a recession year, and climbed back to only 66 million in 1961. U.S. Steel, in actuality, was yielding to increasingly formidable competition from both American and foreign steel-producers. Newer domestic companies like the Inland Steel Company, the Kaiser Steel Corporation, and the Armco Steel Corporation were making deep inroads into the steel market. And the growing foreign steel industries, chiefly those of Western Europe, were boasting highly efficient new steel mills with steadily expanding capacity. The impact upon the American steel industry is suggested by these figures: in 1955, the United States exported 4,061,000 net tons of steel products as opposed to 1,989,000 tons in 1961, and it imported only 973,000 tons in 1955 as compared with 3,164,000 tons in 1961. Still another factor was the alternative materials competing with steel in the American economy—aluminum, plastics, and concrete. These were steadily displacing steel in building materials, containers, automobiles, and other products.

Night Watch

As the President's temper subsided in the twilight of April 10, 1962, he and his assembled aides began to consider the measures the Administration might take. It was clear that the Administration would fight, even though

---

* Late in 1962, Bethlehem Steel announced plans to build a Midwestern steel mill as well.

no one felt it necessary to say so. By 8 P.M. decisions were reached, goals and strategies selected. As an immediate objective, the Administration would seek to deter other steel companies from following U.S. Steel's course in raising prices. Several Administration officials even dared to hope that if enough steel companies could be induced to hold the price line, then U.S. Steel might conceivably be forced to rescind its price increase and revert to its former price position.

One chosen strategy called for an open public attack upon U.S. Steel's action. The opportunity would be at hand within a matter of hours. The President's news conference was scheduled for 3:30 the next afternoon, April 11. Thanks to coverage by television and the press, the President's views would be brought almost instantaneously to a nationwide audience.

From the start of his Administration, the news conference has proven a highly effective weapon in the hands of President Kennedy. The customary opening statement the President makes at a news conference has been well exploited for the presentation of truly newsworthy material. Kennedy's responses to reporters' questions have demonstrated a remarkable grasp of governmental detail and imparted zest and excitement to his Administration. The press conference and the informal interview are Kennedy's fortes. His impact diminishes noticeably in set speeches.

Kennedy faces his news conferences only after careful preparation. Although only twenty-five questions or so can be crammed into the allotted half-hour, he typically has answers ready for eighty questions. Like students preparing for an examination, he and his staff try to anticipate the questions that are apt to be asked. On the afternoon before a news conference, his Press Secretary obtains from the departmental information chiefs the benefit of their experience with press queries in the preceding week. On the day of the news conference, the President ordinarily breakfasts with his Press Secretary, Sorensen, Heller, Bundy, and Secretary of State Dean Rusk. This group canvasses questions that occur to its members and supplies the President with data.

Despite his success with the news conference, Kennedy has used the device erratically. Periods of three and four weeks have passed when he has not met with the press. The greatest lapses occurred in the two Cuban crises when the President apparently concluded that discussion of those situations would not be helpful and that unstudied remarks might be greatly harmful. In the steel dispute, however, the President viewed his coming news conference as an ideal occasion for placing his views before the public.

Material would be needed for the President's opening statement at the April 11 news conference, and Goldberg, Heller, and Sorensen agreed to do the chore. The group recognized that specially prepared statistical data would be required in a longer-term effort to refute the case for the price increase.

As discussion proceeded, the President occasionally withdrew to his telephone. He called his brother Robert, Secretary of Defense McNamara, and Secretary of the Treasury Dillon, then vacationing in Florida. At his home in northwest Washington, Senator Estes Kefauver, Democrat of Tennessee, chairman of the Senate Antitrust Subcommittee, was preparing to go out for the evening when his phone rang. It was the President. Would the Senator publicly express "dismay" over the price rise and consider an investigation? The response was affirmative, as the President had every reason to expect. Intermittently over the preceding five years, Senator Kefauver had been investigating steel-pricing practices and making findings critical of the industry.

As the President telephoned, his aides considered the economic rebuttal of U.S. Steel's case needed for the news conference. How could the necessary data be best prepared? Goldberg's and Heller's agencies, which had the most economists and statisticians familiar with the steel situation, decided to pool their staff resources. A staff group was hastily assembled in Heller's office. He worked with them briefly before hurrying off to a dinner in honor of Professor Walter Hallstein, president of the European Common Market.

Heller was not the only member of this small group who had to subordinate high-policy concerns to social necessity. Back at the White House, the President had donned formal clothes for his annual reception for members of Congress and their wives. Occasionally, through the evening, Kennedy would slip out to talk about steel. Since the reception was spread over three rooms, he could easily come and go. He finally left the reception about midnight and immediately retired. His aides of the White House Staff, the Council of Economic Advisers, and the Departments of Labor, Defense, Justice, Commerce, and the Treasury, however, were furiously at work preparing the counterattack.

Wednesday, April 11

Reactions
Shortly after midnight, Heller returned from the evening's banquet to his office, accompanied by a fellow guest, George W. Ball, Undersecretary of State. On hand in Heller's office were his two CEA colleagues, Gordon and Tobin, and the group from the Bureau of Labor Statistics. At about 2:45 A.M. the Labor group left the session, bearing an assignment to convert a fact book on steel prepared by the Eisenhower Administration two years before into a kind of "white paper" demonstrating that the price increase was unjustified. Finally, at 4 A.M. the CEA members quit their toil. Heller and Tobin went home for several hours sleep, and Gordon took to a couch in his office.

As the regular workday commenced, the President held a breakfast meeting at the White House with Vice-President Lyndon Johnson, Secretary of State Rusk—who apparently played no part in the steel crisis—Goldberg, Sorensen, Sorensen's deputy Myer Feldman, Heller, and Hatcher. The meeting, which lasted an hour and forty-five minutes, heard a report from Goldberg and Heller on the previous night's work. Sorensen was asked to draft the President's statement on steel for the news conference.

During the morning in his office, the President called Secretary Dillon in Florida to discuss the Treasury's preparation of legislation for more liberal tax write-offs to encourage the modernization of plant and machinery. It was agreed that the price crisis should not slow or alter the tax project. The President also telephoned Secretary Hodges to open a new phase of the strategy to prevent other steel companies from raising prices.

On Capitol Hill, the initial reaction was pleasing to the Administration. The Democratic leadership and even party members with a broad streak of independence were backing up the President. Mike Mansfield, Senate majority leader, called the price increase "unjustified"; to Speaker John W. McCormack it was "shocking," "arrogant," and "irresponsible." Senator Hubert H. Humphrey of Minnesota, Democratic whip, called it "an affront to the President." Senator Kefauver and Congressman Emanuel Celler of Brooklyn, chairmen of the Senate and House Antitrust Subcommittees, respectively, announced the scheduling of broad investigations of the steel industry. On the Senate floor, Albert Gore, Democrat of Tennessee, proposed a law that would empower the courts to prohibit price increases in basic industries such as steel before a prescribed "cooling-off period" had elapsed.

In the Executive Branch, several investigational arms began stirring. The earlier White House discussions had not overlooked the fact that there were certain punitive laws on the books that could conceivably be applied to U.S. Steel and its price action to deter other steel companies from doing likewise. The most serviceable of these laws were the Sherman Antitrust Act, the Clayton Antitrust Act, and the Federal Trade Commission Act, plus various amendments and extensions. This statutory complex is collectively known as "the Antitrust Laws." The Antitrust Division of the Justice Department, a spokesman for Attorney General Kennedy said, was taking "an immediate and close look" at industry developments before and after U.S. Steel's announcement of a price increase to determine whether the Clayton or Sherman Acts had been violated. At the Federal Trade Commission, a companion move was launched when Paul Rand Dixon, chairman, said that the FTC had begun an informal inquiry that might eventuate in fines of up to $5,000 a day for violation of its consent order of June 15, 1961. (A "consent order" is a settlement out of court in which a private company or several companies agree to refrain from certain practices which in the view of the FTC violate the Antitrust Laws.) The consent order of June 15 had been requested by certain steel companies, following an FTC complaint, and it bound the entire steel industry to refrain from collusive price-fixing or maintaining identical delivered prices.

The Case for U.S. Steel

The morning newspapers of April 11 featured U.S. Steel's announcement that as of midnight, April 10, steel prices would average an across-the-board increase of $6 a ton. The company said the increase would affect all its principal products, including those of its three operating divisions— American Steel and Wire, National Tube, and Tennessee Coal and Iron. The increase of $6 a ton was in actuality a sizable one, standing midway between the biggest and smallest of the ten postwar steel price increases.

U.S. Steel's announcement was accompanied by an extended statement of justification by its president, Leslie B. Worthington. As the price dispute developed, additional statements by company officials enlarged upon the company's case. Since 1958, U.S. Steel argued, the level of steel prices had remained stable in the face of four increases in steelworker wages, rising state and local taxes, interest on borrowings, the costs of products and services the company used, and growing competitive pressure from low-cost foreign mills and alternative domestic materials. To face its competition, U.S. Steel needed to modernize, for which it needed funds. Existing profits, squeezed between rising costs and stable prices, could not provide them.

Since 1958, U.S. Steel had spent $1.19 billion for the modernization and replacement of facilities and for the development of new sources of raw materials. These improvements had been financed through profits and $800 million in borrowings. Both the further improvements that were badly needed and the repayment of past borrowings depended on future profits, and here, U.S. Steel said, was the rub. Profits after the payment of dividends had declined from $115 million in 1958 to less than $3 million in 1961. (The dividend rate had not been increased during the past five years.) The path to higher profits was via higher, more realistic prices. The price increase just invoked was patently a modest one.

Altogether, U.S. Steel had suffered a net increase in costs of about 6 per cent from 1958 to 1961. Therefore, the newly announced price increase of 3.5 per cent, the company contended, "clearly falls considerably short of the amount needed to restore even the cost-price relationship in the low production year of 1958."

U.S. Steel emphasized that the increase of $6 per ton or .3 cent per pound in the price of steel "adds almost negligibly to the cost of the steel which goes into the familiar, everyday products that we use." Thus it contended that the price of a refrigerator would rise only 65 cents; a domestic gas range, 70 cents; a wringer-type washing machine, 35 cents; a toaster, 3 cents; a small car, $6.83; an intermediate-size one, $8.33; and a standard-size one, $10.64.

U.S. Steel spokesmen also referred to a study made in 1960 by Professor E. Robert Livernash of the Harvard Business School at the request of Secretary of Labor James P. Mitchell. The Livernash report concluded: "The exploratory analysis undertaken in this study suggests that the independent influence of steel prices on inflation has been modest in the postwar period."

Presidential Economics

President Kennedy and his aides started from different premises about the nature and consequences of steel prices. Their increase, the Administration was convinced, would touch off a ripple of price rises spreading throughout the economy on commodities ranging from kitchen knives to bridge beams. Support for this view was provided by a much-quoted 1959 study by Professors Otto Eckstein and Garry Fromm of Harvard University for the Joint Economic Committee of Congress. The Eckstein study concluded that the impact of steel price increases on other industrial prices is "large." If steel prices had behaved like other industrial prices, they found, the rise in the total wholesale price index would have been 40 per cent less over the 1949–59 decade and 52 per cent less since 1953. The increase in the price of finished goods would have been 23 and 38 per cent less, respectively.

The Kennedy Administration's opposition to a price increase was also predicated upon certain statistical interpretations of steel economics. From 1958, the year of steel's last price rise, to 1961, the hourly wage and fringe-benefit costs per worker had risen 12.8 per cent, and the hourly output per worker 12.6 per cent. If a worker's output rate has risen as much as the rate of his pay, the Administration reasoned, the labor cost of what he now produces is "essentially the same," or an infinitesimal .2 per cent more.

As to the labor-cost outlook under the 1962 labor-management steel contract, the Kennedy Administration calculated that if the steel industry's productivity continued to improve at a rate of about 3.5 per cent a year, as it had between 1958 and 1962, this alone would more than cover the newly negotiated 10-cent-an-hour increase in fringe benefits. Hence the President had hailed the contract as "noninflationary."

On the issue of the inadequate profits that President Worthington had complained of in his Chicago speech, the Administration started from premises different from those of the company. The question was not, the Administration felt, whether profits were adequate or inadequate under existing costs and prices. What really mattered was that profits were declining because of slack business—not because of increased costs and unduly low prices. Steel industry operations averaged two-thirds or less of capacity in the 1957–61 period. The Administration estimated that if operations rose to 90 per cent of capacity, industry profits would yield a sensational 13.5 per cent return on capital. The Kennedy Administration's attitude on steel profits was also affected by its findings that the steel industry was not the only one suffering from less-than-capacity business. The pattern was rather general in the American industrial economy. The Administration felt that increased demand could provide both greater profits for business and greater income for labor.

The Administration also rejected steel's argument that it needed higher prices to finance new investment in more efficient plant and equipment. The latter could be achieved through the "investment credit" provision of a tax bill the Administration was sponsoring to encourage industrial modernization. Under the bill's provisions, the steel industry would save $110 million in 1962, and U.S. Steel alone would save $35 million—a sum that would become, in effect, an annual source of capital for the company.

The Reaction of the Steel Community

U.S. Steel's price action evidently came as a surprise to the other major steel companies. Communication clearly seemed lacking between Bethlehem Steel, the nation's second largest producer, and U.S. Steel. At a stockholders' meeting in Wilmington, Delaware, on April 10, Bethlehem's President Edmund F. Martin was reported to have said that the new labor contract should not occasion a price rise. "We should not do anything to increase our costs if we are to survive," he explained. "We have more competition both domestically and from foreign firms. And we need to sell more steel."

The heads of several major steel companies, when apprised of U.S. Steel's action, were unanimously sympathetic. William A. Stelle, for example, president of the Wheeling Steel Company, eleventh largest steel producer, said the price boost was "long overdue." His company, however, he said, would have to study the situation before deciding what to do. T. F. Patton, president of the Republic Steel Corporation of Cleveland, the third largest producer, was more positive. "Republic certainly needs a price increase," he said. "We will review the reported action of United States Steel immediately."

Bethlehem Does It Too

President Kennedy's hope that other steel companies would abstain from following U.S. Steel's lead was severely jolted. At noon, when the President emerged from the White House to welcome the Shah and Empress of Iran at the airport for several days' visit, he was handed a news bulletin that Bethlehem Steel was also boosting its prices. President Martin, notwithstanding the contrary sentiments attributed to him at Wilmington, had evidently changed his mind. Bethlehem's price rise was similar in size and coverage to U.S. Steel's. If Mr. Kennedy had not headed off for the airport, he would have received further news bulletins minutes later announcing that several other major steel companies, including Republic Steel, were following Bethlehem's and U.S. Steel's examples. From two of the companies the Administration was heavily counting on to resist the swelling trend came only inscrutable fence-straddling statements. The Kaiser Steel Corporation said, "We're studying the subject in the light of our own competitive situation." John F. Smith, Jr., president of the Inland Steel Company, announced that his company "will reserve its decision on what action to take until we are more completely informed. We will . . . give the matter very careful study. . . ."

Presidential Anger

The President, arriving for his 3:30 news conference one minute late, strode quickly to the lectern in the State Department auditorium and, in tones of "cold anger" (a favorite press phrase), read a lengthy indictment of the price-boosting steel companies. At a time of grave crisis in Berlin and Southeast Asia, when servicemen were being asked to risk their lives, reservists to leave their families, and union members to hold down their wage requests, when restraint and sacrifice were asked of every citizen, Kennedy said, he found it hard "to accept a situation in which a tiny handful of steel executives" could show "such utter contempt for the interest of 185,000,000 Americans."

The President listed some anticipated consequences of the price rise: its general inflationary effect upon the economy, a $1 billion rise in defense costs, a worsening of the nation's balance-of-payments position and the competitive capacity of its goods in foreign trade. The President spoke in unremittingly angry tones and jabbed with his forefinger for emphasis. An atmosphere of intensity pervaded the auditorium from the opening statement through the reporters' questioning. Of seventeen questions asked, nine concerned the steel situation.

In his responses, the President said that in view of the "speedy action" of other steel companies "who have entirely different economic problems facing them than did United States Steel," the Justice Department was anxious to determine whether any laws had been violated.

Several reporters' questions and the President's answers filled in some of the gaps in the public's knowledge of the earlier stages of the steel events and illuminated the Administration's attitude toward past and possible future moves.

> Q: In your conversation with Mr. Blough yesterday, did you make a direct request that this price increase be either deferred or rescinded?
> A: . . . I told Mr. Blough of my very keen disappointment and what I thought would be the most unfortunate effects of it. . . .
> Q: . . . Is the position of the Administration that it believed it had the assurance of the steel industry at the time of the recent labor agreement that it would not increase prices?
> A: We did not ask either side to give us any assurance, . . . because

there is a very proper limitation to the power of the Government in this free economy.

All we did in our meetings was to emphasize how important it was that . . . there be price stability, and we stressed that our whole purpose in attempting to persuade the union to begin to bargain early and to make an agreement which would not affect prices, of course, was for the purpose of maintaining price stability.

That was the thread that ran through every discussion which I had, or Secretary Goldberg.

Q: Mr. President, two years ago, after the settlement, I believe steel prices were not raised. Do you think there was an element of political discrimination in the behavior of the industry this year?

A: I would not . . . if that was the purpose . . . the country's the one that suffers. . . . If they do it in order to spite me it really isn't so important.

Steel-Users

Beyond the immediate circle of the steel industry, the American business community reacted to the price increase with mingled surprise, anxiety, and approval. Some steel-users feared that the price rises would intensify their competitive problems. According to the *Wall Street Journal* of April 12, several users who had never bought low-priced foreign steel were now considering it. Others were planning to replace steel altogether. Building contractors were thinking of using more concrete. A maker of prefabricated roofs was beholding aluminum more fondly. The Whirlpool Corporation, a major manufacturer of kitchen equipment, was eying plastic parts for appliances with quickened interest. The Zebco Company of Tulsa, Oklahoma, a maker of fishing reels and a subsidiary of the Brunswick Corporation, announced that it "will definitely be going more and more to plastics and aluminum." (Zebco was already making 50 per cent of its reels from plastics in 1962, compared with 2 per cent in 1949.)

Several aspects of the steel move baffled the business community. Its timing was puzzling. Coming hard on the heels of the new labor contract, at a moment when the Kennedy Administration was elated at warding off its potential inflationary threat, U.S. Steel's decision doused the happy mood with ice water. The manner of U.S. Steel's action seemed almost calculated to produce maximum political anger. The economic rationale of the move also seemed obscure. For weeks prior to the negotiation of the labor contract, steel-users had built up large inventories as a hedge against a possible strike. But the strike had not materialized and steel-users now found themselves saddled with bulging inventories to work off. Even before the price increase, a drop in steel orders and therefore in production was becoming apparent. In a sense, the price rise was redundant. It would merely make doubly sure that an already declining market would be more than a transient phenomenon.

The preliminary evidence indicated that the steel rise would touch off a general price increase. Of fifty steel-using companies queried on their future pricing plans, thirty-five replied that they expected to raise prices in coming months. In some instances, the increase would be larger than the rise in steel alone would warrant. "It's a good reason for passing on an accumulation of other rising costs, mostly labor," said Henry Wilson, president of H. & H. Wilson, Inc., Los Angeles, a maker of milling machines.

Some steel-users were fearful that the price increase would cut into their profits. "We stand to lose maybe $150,000 that will come out of our pockets in gross profits on just those steel orders we have on the books now," said John E. Beall, president of the Beall Pipe & Tank Corporation, a Portland, Oregon, steel fabricator. Beall could not raise prices on orders already booked.

But even those steel-users who stood to suffer from U.S. Steel's price increase perceived a silver lining in the massive clouds. These users beheld U.S. Steel's action as a business declaration of independence from political pressure. They were elated that in the face of President Kennedy's several admonitions against price rises, U.S. Steel had seemingly dared to make itself something of a profile in courage by defying the Administration's strictures and boldly recouping its growing costs.

Divide and Conquer

After the first wave of price increases, CEA members Heller and Gordon began to evaluate the results. Five companies of the so-called Big Twelve—the Inland Steel Company, the Armco Steel Corporation, the McLouth Steel Corporation, the Colorado Fuel and Iron Corporation, and the Kaiser Steel Corporation—had not yet raised their prices. By now, a rough distinction between the type of steel company that had raised prices and the type that had not was beginning to suggest a possible Administration strategy. Those companies that had raised prices, exemplified by U.S. Steel, tended to be older companies with conservative leadership and larger but less efficient operations. In recent years, these companies have been slow to adjust to changing market conditions. In the later 1950's, customer demand changed from low-profit heavy products, in which U.S. Steel's capacity was concentrated, to high-profit light ones. While various other steel companies drastically revamped their product mix to take advantage of the demand for lighter steel, U.S. Steel did not. In 1962, only 20 per cent of its capacity was devoted to light flat-rolled steels. In effect, U.S. Steel was tenaciously banking on heavy steels for capital-goods industries while the competition was emphasizing lighter steels for the growing market of containers, appliances, and automobiles. Light flat-rolled products were expected to constitute half of all steel shipments in 1962.

The older steel companies had a long tradition of controversy with government when it intervened in their affairs. In the 1930's, the Jones & Laughlin Steel Corporation battled the National Labor Relations Board in the United States Supreme Court; the Youngstown Sheet and Tube Company defeated Truman's attempted seizure of the steel mills in 1952.

A second type of steel company is represented by newer and more efficient companies. Illustrative of this type is Inland Steel of Chicago, the nation's eighth largest producer. Inland's 1961 profit margin of 7.5 per cent of sales topped all seven of its larger competitors, and it also had the best return on investment. In a tradition-bound industry that accords great weight to production and finance, Inland has given exceptional attention to sales. Its strategy of frequently interrupting production schedules to rush out small orders for users who needed steel fast was virtually unheard of. "The whole blamed outfit is run by sales people," said an official of a major competitor, "so naturally they are more flexible than we are." In planning production, Inland makes a noticeably faster response to the changing demand situation than most competitors. "Inland doesn't bother with the cats and dogs in the product mix," said a steel executive of another company. "For instance," he explained, "when rails, axles, and wheels faded in popularity a few years ago, Inland didn't take long to get out of that business and into wide-flange beams that were more profitable." The newer companies tend also to be alert to technological advance. In 1962, one of these, the Lukens Steel Company, introduced a major new line of superior-strength carbon steels, with higher strength levels and savings of 15 per cent in material costs.

In addition, these companies are characterized by a reputation for "public mindedness." Clarence B. Randall, a former chairman of the board at Inland, served in key posts in the Eisenhower and Kennedy Administrations. Joseph Leopold Block, the company's present chairman, was a member of President Kennedy's Labor-Management Advisory Committee, president of the Chicago Community Fund, and a former dollar-a-year man for the War Production Board in World War II. (At this juncture in the price crisis, Joseph Block was in Japan.) Another of these companies, Kaiser Steel—described by the New York *Times* as "long a maverick in the industry"—has often taken a more progressive view than the rest of the industry on questions of labor relations and price policies.

Economists Heller and Gordon argued that with more efficient plant facilities, these holdout companies like Inland could clear a profit at lower prices while increasing their sales volume at the expense of the higher-priced companies. The five holdouts represented 14 per cent of the total industry's capacity and 17 per cent of the Big Twelve's. If the Administration could convince these five companies not to raise prices, Heller and Gordon predicted that they would soon be doing 25 per cent of the national steel business. And given the adverse conditions of the steel market, higher-priced sellers would be forced to rescind.

It was in hopeful pursuance of this "divide-and-conquer" strategy that Edward Gudeman, Undersecretary of Commerce, telephoned Philip D. Block, Inland's vice-chairman, at 7:45 Wednesday morning. Gudeman was a friend and former classmate of Block's.

"What do you think of this price increase of United States Steel?" asked Gudeman.

Block said he had been surprised.

"I didn't ask P. D. what Inland might do," Gudeman said afterward. "I didn't want them to feel that the Administration was putting them on the spot. I just wanted him to know how we felt and to ask his consideration."

Gudeman's call was followed by one from Henry H. Fowler, Undersecretary of the Treasury, to John F. Smith, Jr., Inland's president, and another from Secretary Goldberg to Leigh B. Block, vice-president for purchasing. Both callers adopted the "soft-sell" manner.

The Administration's endeavors to wean away the steel companies from the price increase were by no means limited to Inland. Kaiser Steel and Armco Steel were also courted in the established style. President Kennedy himself talked to Edgar Kaiser, chairman of Kaiser Steel, in California, and Secretary McNamara called friends at a number of companies, including the Allegheny Ludlum Steel Corporation, a leading manufacturer of stainless and specialty steel.

There was a further step, with a sharper edge than the friendly phone call. Administration officials put in a number of calls to steel-users around the country, urging them in turn to telephone their friends among the steelmakers and explain their feelings concerning the price increase and, if possible, to issue suitable public statements.

The Antitrust Weapon

Concurrently with its "divide-and-conquer" maneuver, the Administration was moving ahead on its antitrust push. Presumably, by brandishing the big stick of antitrust, the Administration might scare off other steel companies from joining the price-hike parade, and hopefully, steel companies already committed to the price rise might reconsider the step. Interest in the antitrust move soared when an Administration official spotted in the Wednesday morning newspapers the statement at Wilmington attributed to Edmund F. Martin, president of Bethlehem Steel, opposing any price increase. The Martin statement made the Justice Department's antitrust specialists prick up their ears. If Martin had opposed a price rise on Tuesday, before U.S. Steel announced its increase, and if Bethlehem Steel raised its prices on Wednesday, after that announcement, Martin's statement might prove significant in antitrust proceedings. It could support a possible government argument that U.S. Steel exercised undue influence over other steel-producers because of its size.

At about six o'clock Wednesday evening, Attorney General Kennedy ordered the Federal Bureau of Investigation to find out as exactly as possible what Mr. Martin had said. Almost simultaneously, FTC Chairman Paul Rand Dixon announced to the press that the FTC was beginning an informal investigation to determine whether the steel companies had violated the consent decree of June 15, 1961 (mentioned earlier).

Friendly Persuasion

The Administration's attack had still another dimension. A sizable effort was afoot to mobilize friendly forces in the political world and in the business community that stretched beyond the immediate sector of steel-producers and users. The technique was the same as before: the friendly low-key telephone call from Washington.

At the Democratic National Committee headquarters, calls were made to many Democratic governors across the nation, including David L. Lawrence of Pennsylvania, Richard J. Hughes of New Jersey, and Edmund G. Brown of California. Do two things, the Governors were asked. Make public statements supporting the President, and request steel-makers in your state to hold the price line. The Democratic Committee spokesmen meticulously abstained from making any statement in the name of the Committee. The Administration's campaign could not be tarnished by the slightest suggestion of "politics."

As afternoon yielded to twilight, the Administration's multiple strategies were in full operation. Here and there a major telephone call had to be made, like that of Undersecretary of the Treasury Robert V. Roosa to Henry Alexander, chairman of the Morgan Guaranty Trust Company in New York. Morgan Guaranty is represented on the board of directors of U.S. Steel and is considered a most powerful influence upon the corporation in the business community.

In early evening, President and Mrs. Kennedy gave a state dinner in honor of the visiting Shah and Empress of Iran. But after the guests had gone, the President returned to his telephone to put in a person-to-person call to Archibald Cox, Solicitor General of the United States, in Tucson, Arizona. The call went through at 12:15 A.M.

Thursday, April 12

The FBI Goes Calling

Solicitor General Cox had flown to Tucson Wednesday afternoon where he was to make two speeches to the Arizona bar. When the telephone rang, the President, who practices and expects conciseness, came right to the point. What suggestions did Cox have for rolling back steel prices? It was not amiss to put so vital a question to the Solicitor General. A Harvard

Law School professor on leave, Cox was Wage Stabilization Board chairman during the Korean War and had worked with Kennedy the Senator on statements on past steel strikes and price disputes. After the President's call, the Solicitor General stayed up all night, thinking and making notes. As the hours slipped by, Cox concluded that the existing antitrust laws could not cope with the steel problem and that special legislation would be necessary. He began to set out on paper the fragments of a legislative draft.

Archibald Cox was not the only American sacrificing his sleep to the steel problem. The FBI was also on the job. At 3 A.M. Lee Linder, a reporter in the Philadelphia bureau of the Associated Press, was awakened by his ringing telephone. Linder had attended the Bethlehem stockholders' meeting in Wilmington, Delaware, Tuesday and with two other reporters had talked with Bethlehem's President Martin after the meeting. It was Linder who had reported the prized quotation attributed to Martin. When Linder answered his phone at 3 A.M. and demanded with sleepy peevishness to know whom he was talking to, the response was clear and jolting. It was the FBI. It was a hoax, thought Linder, and he put down the receiver. Just to make sure, he called the FBI. The agents indeed were serious. He was asked a question or two on the telephone and was then told that several lawmen were "coming right out to see you."

Within a half-hour, the FBI was at Linder's door. What did he know about the Bethlehem president's statement? Linder repeated what he had written for the Associated Press.

The FBI also caught up with two other reporters who had talked to Martin after the Wilmington meeting. At 5 A.M., the FBI reached the second reporter, John Lawrence of the *Wall Street Journal.* "I told them I had nothing to say, so they gave up," said Lawrence of his encounter with the FBI. And when the third reporter, James L. Parks, Jr., of the Wilmington *Evening Journal,* arrived at his office at 6:30 A.M., two FBI agents were there waiting for him.

When the FBI's visitations to the newspapermen became known, an outcry of criticism was heard in several places. Among the first to protest was Congressman William E. Miller of upstate New York, chairman of the Republican National Committee. Until this point, Republicans had maintained an embarrassed silence on the steel controversy, but the FBI episode presented an irresistible opportunity. Congressman Miller attributed the FBI action to Attorney General Robert Kennedy's own instigation. "This is reminiscent of the days of Hitler when the German people lived in fear of the knock on the door in the middle of the night," exclaimed Miller. It was "a sinister and apprehensive development," he continued, "when the nation's Attorney General uses the chief law enforcement arm of the Government to pursue a political issue. This is but a short step away from the police state—a breakdown in the sanctity of the American form of government." The Justice Department had no comment.

Ferment

As the day proceeded, the several centers of decision operated at accelerated tempo. In Chicago, Philip Block and two other high officials of Inland Steel reached a decision: prices would not be raised. They called Joseph Block in Japan, and he concurred. All agreed that a directors' meeting should be arranged to ratify the decision the next morning. Meanwhile, no announcement was to go out, and no one in Washington was to be told of the decision. As Inland was making up its mind, two other steel companies were announcing $6-a-ton price increases: the National Steel Corporation, fifth largest producer, and the Pittsburgh Steel Company, fourteenth largest producer.

The Kennedy Administration found comfort in Inland's continued silence and in a report from Kaiser Steel that it was "still studying the situation, relative to our competitive position in the market." Asked when a decision might be expected, a Kaiser spokesman said, "None appears imminent."

President Kennedy himself summoned various department and subdepartment heads and White House assistants to an early-morning meeting in the cabinet room. Among those present at the forty-five-minute session were Attorney General Kennedy, Secretary of Defense McNamara, Labor Secretary Goldberg, Commerce Secretary Hodges, Treasury Undersecretary Fowler, CEA Chairman Heller, FTC Chairman Dixon, and Sorensen, the President's Special Counsel. The group discussed their next moves. The President attended the meeting for fifteen minutes and then left for talks with the Shah of Iran.

Throughout the morning, Administration officials maintained a steady volley of public statements underscoring the magnitude of the crisis. William P. Bundy, Deputy Assistant Secretary of Defense for International Security Affairs, testified before the Senate Foreign Relations Committee that the steel increase would raise the cost of military foreign aid in the next fiscal year by $50 million to $75 million. Frank M. Coffin, Deputy Foreign Aid Administrator in Charge of Development, estimated that the cost of economic aid would be increased by $6 million to $10 million. Another Foreign Relations Committee witness, Undersecretary of State George W. Ball, recalled the great alarm expressed "in some quarters" that the recently negotiated concessions to the Common Market on specialty steel products would damage the domestic industry. With heavy irony the Undersecretary added, "I can only assume from the action taken monolithically in this case (of the steel increase) that the steel industry doesn't have any concern about competitive steel imports."

Not all the verbal fusillade in Washington was devoted to the Administration's cause. In their weekly news conference, held also in the morning, the Republican Congressional leaders, Senator Everett M. Dirksen of Illinois and Congressman Charles A. Halleck of Indiana, countered the President's contention that the steel increase was inflationary. Senator Dirksen, who neither approved nor condemned the increase, said the President was "looking in the wrong place" for the basic cause of inflation. "The prime factor in inflation is excessive Government spending," said the Senator.

In New York, another scheduled news conference—Roger M. Blough's—was awaited with high interest. He would make a prepared statement, it was announced, and answer questions. The proceedings would be carried on television and radio from U.S. Steel's auditorium at 71 Broadway. The occasion had been hurriedly arranged after President Kennedy's lamentation of the price increase in his news conference the day before.

Roger Blough's News Conference

At 3:30 P.M., Roger Blough commenced his news conference, flanked by President Worthington and General Counsel John S. Tennant. Blough spoke into a battery of microphones and looked beyond to some ninety-five newsmen and as many photographers and technicians. He conducted the hour-long affair in a sober and restrained manner until he was asked if political considerations had played a part in the decision to raise prices Tuesday rather than during the Republican Administration of former President Eisenhower. "I think you gentlemen can readily see that I know nothing about politics," Blough replied, drawing laughter from the crowd.

His presentation entailed a lengthy prepared statement pointing out that President Kennedy's remarks yesterday had led to today's conference, and there was not, on the company's part, any desire to add to already existing acrimony or misunderstanding. But he said, "Neither do we believe that anyone can properly assume that we are less concerned with the welfare, the strength and the vitality of this nation than are those who have criticized our action."

Upon completing his statement, Blough took up questions from the floor:

Q: . . . Would you accept some sort of an independent study of the merits of your cost-squeeze state?

A: . . . Well, I don't know under what circumstances that study would be made. . . . I really believe that it's quite important in the kind of society that we have that individual companies, in as highly competitive an industry as we have, and in every industry for that matter, should make their own pricing decisions.

Q: Can you foresee any changes in the tax laws or any changes in depreciation allowances that would permit you to reconsider the price rise?

A: . . . This problem as related to pricing is a continuous thing. If all the factors that are involved in decision making are taken into account, time after time over many years, if there are changes in the tax laws that are beneficial from the standpoint of depreciation, which is certainly something that's needed, that would for sure be a factor that would be taken into account so far as we're concerned.

Q: Do you feel, in the light of what's happened . . . that perhaps you could have given him [President Kennedy] a little more advance notice than you actually did?

A: Well, of course I'm quite concerned at the President's concern. In the kind of an economy that we have, I'm not quite sure that it's feasible for anyone to be going to the White House to consider a price increase, even as important a one as this . . . .

Q: . . . If [Armco, Inland and other steel companies that haven't raised their prices] don't go along, how long can you stick to your price increase before you have to rescind it?

A: It definitely would affect us and I don't know how long we could maintain our position.

Blows Against U.S. Steel

In his response to questions, Blough confirmed that the antitrust strategy, fashioned in the Justice Department, had now been launched. The U.S. Steel chairman acknowledged that the corporation had been served with a subpoena, returnable in the Federal District Court for the Southern District of New York, to "produce some papers."

At 7 P.M., Attorney General Robert F. Kennedy made his expected announcement that he had ordered a grand-jury investigation of the price increases of the leading steel-makers. Evidence, he said, would be presented to a grand jury then sitting in New York. Some hours before the Attorney General's statement, Justice Department agents appeared at the headquarters of not only U.S. Steel but also Bethlehem Steel, Jones & Laughlin Steel, and other companies to serve subpoenas for documents bearing on the price increase and other matters. The Attorney General's announcement came as the Kennedys were preparing for another state dinner with the Shah and Empress, this time at the Iranian Embassy.

The Attorney General rested his order for a grand-jury investigation on Sections 1 and 2 of the Sherman Antitrust Act. Section 1 forbids unreasonable restraint of trade, including combination or conspiracy to fix prices. Section 2 forbids attempts to establish or conduct a monopoly. Under Section 2, the government would be expected to show that a given corporation is so large in its field that it exercises coercive power upon other companies in the same industry. A grand-jury investigation implies scrutiny for criminality and not merely civil action.

FBI agents were not the only government visitors in New York that Mr. Blough and his colleagues had to cope with. About ten minutes after the Blough press conference had begun, Secretary of Commerce Hodges arrived at the University Club in New York. It had been decided at the morning White House meeting that the Administration should make a swift point-by-point rebuttal to Blough's presentation; Secretary Hodges was chosen to do the job. His press conference in New York was scheduled for 5 P.M. While he shaved and changed his shirt, his assistant, William M. Ruder, tried to take notes on the Blough broadcast. Ruder's assignment was unenviable, for the static on the radio he was using crackled like a well-scratched phonograph.

Secretary Hodges held his news conference promptly at 5 P.M. in the Empire State Building. He warned that the steel price increase might set off an inflationary spiral that would injure domestic business as well as the country's international balance-of-payments position. (One-third of our exports, he pointed out, were of products making heavy use of steel.) Hodges charged that Blough, while alluding to rising labor costs in his news conference, had failed to "mention the corresponding rise in productivity." In addition, Blough's contention that the price increase was needed to modernize plant facilities neglected to take into account the bill just passed by the House of Representatives providing for a tax credit for modernization that in the case of U.S. Steel would amount to $35 million. The company also had prospects of an additional $10 million through a newly increased depreciation allowance. ("Depreciation" is an accounting classification sanctioned by the Internal Revenue Service. It is an account into which a company may put revenue to replace worn-out machinery. Funds in such accounts are not taxable. Therefore, a liberalization of depreciation regulations affecting the steel industry means that the Internal Revenue Service enlarges its definition of "depreciation" to permit the steel companies to shunt more revenues into tax-free accounts. Steel companies would consequently be able to pay less in taxes to the federal government.)

Far more damaging to U.S. Steel's case than Hodges' rebuttal was the telegram to Blough of two leading Pennsylvania Republicans, Congressmen William W. Scranton and James E. Van Zandt, urging reconsideration of the price increase. Scranton and Van Zandt indeed were more than Congressmen. They were respectively the gubernatorial and Senatorial nominees of the state Republican organization in the approaching 1962 elections. The Scranton–Van Zandt telegram was unsparing. The price increase at this time "was wrong," it read, "—wrong for Pennsylvania, wrong for America, wrong for the free world. The increase surely will set off another round of inflation. It will hurt people most who can least afford to be hurt."

The Secret Phase

The Kennedy Administration's efforts now passed into a new and secret phase. While the competing press conferences and the grand-jury investigation were dominating newspaper headlines, two secret moves of considerable potentiality were under way.

Of the first move, very little is known. It involved a newspaperman, Charles L. Bartlett, Washington correspondent of the Chattanooga *Times,* whose only comment has been, "I helped two friends get in touch with each other again." President Kennedy presumably was one of these friends, since Mr. Bartlett and his wife are members of the Kennedy social set. The other friend was an officer of U.S. Steel whose identity has not yet been established, but by every indication it was Blough whom Bartlett also knows. Apparently Bartlett sought to reopen "diplomatic relations" between his Washington and New York friends, although the degree of his success remains shrouded in carefully guarded obscurity. A cabinet member, however, has vouchsafed that it was "useful."

Of the second secret initiative, more is known. It was conceivably an offspring of the first. Toward noon on Thursday, the President telephoned Clark Clifford, a Washington lawyer who was once prominent as the President's Special Counsel in the Truman Administration and as a leading strategist in Truman's extraordinary 1948 campaign. President Kennedy came quickly to the point. Secretary Goldberg, he said, knew the officers of U.S. Steel very well, and could, of course, talk to them on the Administration's behalf. A difficulty was that as former counsel to the Steelworkers union, Goldberg was known to the steel executives mainly as an adversary. Through his private law practice, Clifford, the President pointed out, enjoyed wide acquaintance with corporation executives and understood their thinking. Would Clifford join Goldberg in talking with U.S. Steel? Clifford would indeed.

He flew to New York and met Chairman Blough, presenting himself as a friend of the disputants. Frankly declaring his complete agreement with President Kennedy's position, Clifford explained that he was seeking to help rectify a tragic mistake, committed, to be sure, by U.S. Steel. Clifford launched into an analysis not unknown to Blough. For fourteen months, said Clifford, the President and Secretary Goldberg had worked for healthy conditions in the steel industry and for an atmosphere of cooperation in the national interest. Unfortunately, this climate had been dissipated by the price increase. Clifford now got down to the delicate, but necessary, task of communicating the President's own views. Mr. Kennedy, said Clifford, believed there had been a dozen or more occasions when the company's leaders could easily have told him that despite all he had done they might have to raise prices. The unsavory, undeniable fact was that they had never told him. Therefore the President had felt double-crossed.

What Blough said in reply to Clifford remains undisclosed. It is known that at the conclusion of their meeting Blough said he would welcome further talks and hoped that Clifford would share in them. Clifford flew back to Washington.

Friday, April 13

News from Inland

The Shah of Iran declared in an address at the National Press Club in Washington, on the last day of his visit, "This king business has given me personally nothing but headaches." Not a few of the Shah's American listeners felt that his remark rang true for their own Chief Executive as well. But there were to be palliatives even for the President. The first news of Friday morning came when Joseph Block of Inland Steel said in Kyoto, Japan, "We do not feel that an advance in steel prices at this time would be in the national interest."

A lengthier statement from Inland's Chicago headquarters at 10:08 A.M. (Washington time) provided a grain of comfort for U.S. Steel, a partial agreement with its basic position. The Inland statement read,

> The company has long recognized the need for improvement in steel industry profits in relation to capital invested. It believes this condition which does exist today will ultimately have to be corrected. Nevertheless, in full recognition of the national interest and competitive factors, the company feels that it is untimely to make any upward adjustments.

President Kennedy learned of the happy news on the steps of the White House as he bade farewell to the Shah of Iran. "Good, good," the President was heard to say. "Very good."

Despite the intoxicating news from Inland, the Kennedy Administration wasted no time in idle jubilation but applied itself relentlessly to the struggle. At 10:15 Solicitor General Cox met in Sorensen's office with a departmental group to consider possible new legislation for the steel problem. Three proposals were put to the group. One called for *ad hoc* legislation limited to the current steel situation, another for permanent legislation imposing some mechanism on wages and prices in the steel industry alone, and the last for permanent legislation setting up "fact-finding" procedures for steel and other basic industries.

At 11:45, Secretary McNamara revealed in a news conference that his department had ordered defense contractors to shift steel purchases to companies that had abstained from raising prices. The announcement of this decision was given further force later in the day when the Defense Department awarded to Lukens Steel, one of the companies that had not raised prices, a contract for more than $5 million worth of a special armor for Polaris-missile submarines. Normally, about half of this order would have gone to U.S. Steel.

At 12:15, President Kennedy and most of his Thursday morning group met again in the cabinet room. Their immediate task was to assess the several new developments in the steel situation that had occurred that morning. Shortly after the news from Inland, Edgar F. Kaiser disclosed in Oakland, California, that Kaiser Steel "will not raise its mill prices at this time." And word came that Armco Steel had also decided to hold the price line but would make no public announcement of its decision. What counted most, however, in this cautiously defined posture, was that Armco was not joining the price revisionists. Inland, Kaiser, and Armco together, the group in the cabinet room estimated, constituted 16 per cent of the nation's steel capacity. While 16 per cent might be enough to force the bigger companies to cancel their price increases, the Administration group concluded that it would be unwise to expect that the retreat would come soon. They laid further plans on the assumption of a prolonged struggle.

As the cabinet group was concluding its deliberations, a report came in of a statement issued in New York by Leonard C. Rose, president of Colorado Fuel and Iron. Rose said that while his company had to consider a price increase in light of rising production costs, it was "studying each of our product lines to determine the feasibility of specific price changes in the light of market conditions." The Rose statement suggested that if Colorado Fuel and Iron moved upward, it might do so only on a selective basis rather than follow U.S. Steel's across-the-board increase.

Conspicuously absent from the gathering in the cabinet room was Secretary Goldberg. He was flying to New York with Clark Clifford in a military air transport for a secret afternoon meeting with Roger Blough and other U.S. Steel officials, including President Worthington and Financial Vice-President Tyson, at the Carlyle Hotel. Again, the President's spokesmen, as in the first meeting, made no demands, threats, or promises.

The deportment of the U.S. Steel officials, according to a participant, was a study in contrasts. They had just received the devastating news of Inland Steel's action. President Worthington "didn't say a word," Financial Vice-President Tyson was "terribly worried," and Chairman Blough was "amiable and tenacious." Most of the meeting was taken up with Blough's defense of the price rise and Goldberg's counterargument. "Did we help you to get a more favorable settlement?" asked Goldberg of the April 6 labor contract that Blough was citing in partial justification for the price rise. Blough answered affirmatively. "Then what do you think we were in there for?" rejoined Goldberg. "Roger, there were eight to ten times during this period when all you had to say was, 'Understand that we are taking part in the negotiations, but understand that no one is going to interfere with our right to raise the price of steel.' Did you ever say that?" Blough acknowledged that he had not, because, he added, he felt it was implicit that steel had the right to raise its prices at any time it chose. Clifford, for his part, contended that U.S. Steel had failed to weigh the consequences of its price rise. If it clung to its new price position, its interest and those of the steel industry would be badly damaged, and the nation as a whole would suffer grievously.

For the men in the Carlyle suite, Inland Steel's decision not to raise prices at the present time made the vital question of future action one of paramount importance. Since Inland would not go along with the price boost, the U.S. Steel executives seemed to assume that their company must inevitably rescind its price rise. The question troubling them most at this juncture was not *whether* the backtracking step should be taken, but rather how could it be managed with a minimum loss of face. "What excuse have we got?" asked Roger Blough. In the ensuing exchange between steel and government officials, three possibilities emerged. First, U.S. Steel could say that further careful study had now shown that the price boost was not in the public interest and thus was being withdrawn. A second possibility was to say there had been a "misunderstanding," and that since the Administration apparently felt so strongly that steel prices should not rise, U.S. Steel would remove the source of controversy and rescind. Finally, U.S. Steel could explain that some steel companies had not gone along with the price increase and that since an intra-industry contest was not in the best interests of the corporation, it was rescinding.

The discussion continued inconclusively until Blough was called to the telephone. Then Goldberg was called. Each received an identical message.

Surrender

The big news that Blough and Goldberg were learning came through at 3:20 P.M. Bethlehem Steel, the number two company in the industry, had rescinded its price increase. It was doing so, in the words of its chairman, Arthur B. Homer, in order "to remain competitive." Homer said,

> Although we still hold the opinion that a steel price increase is needed, under the present conditions, to insure reasonable earnings, to provide the funds necessary to build more competitive facilities, and at least partly to offset the past employment cost increases which have been absorbed without price increases, we must remain competitive. For the ultimate good and future welfare of our economy we must have lower costs to permit lower prices for successful world competition and improved volume of business and employment.

President Kennedy heard the news while flying to Norfolk for a weekend with the fleet. For Kennedy and his Administration colleagues, the Bethlehem development was unexpected.

The Administration had made no special effort to bring Bethlehem around to its decision. The company's price retreat is still something of a mystery, although several explanations have been offered. One supposed factor was the Pentagon's order shifting its steel-buying to mills that did not raise prices. Bethlehem was heavily engaged in shipbuilding, and the Defense Department was its biggest customer. Probably the overriding influence was the fact that Inland was Bethlehem's competitor in the Midwest, where the nation's largest steel market is located. As Joseph Block analyzed the eruptive events of April sometime later on,

> Bethlehem . . . immediately recognized what would happen to them in the national market if they didn't cut prices. In the Chicago area Inland

would be running at full capacity, the rest of the industry at about 50 per cent. To be sure, Chicago is only a part of the national market for steel, but the impact of such action is national, and with the industry only running at 60 per cent nobody could afford to lose any tonnage anywhere.

In addition, many of Inland's customers in Chicago have operations beyond the Chicago marketing area. They could bring heavy pressure in their areas to force prices back to the level Inland maintained in Chicago. Logan T. Johnston, president of Armco, graphically described the situation faced by any price-increasing company. "If we had raised our prices and Inland's stayed put, Inland would have moved so deep into our territory we'd have to put a moat around our plant in Middletown [Ohio] to keep them out."

What would U.S. Steel do now? What could it do? Promptly after the Bethlehem decision, there was a flurry of signals of things to come. One steel executive, whose company had not acted on the question of a price increase yet, had "no comment" when asked what his company might do. Another company executive, whose situation was comparable, had no comment "on anything." In Wall Street, rumors that Blough had resigned as chairman of U.S. Steel began circulating. The company felt compelled to issue a denial, pointing out that Mr. Blough was but fifty-eight years old "and has seven good years to go" before normal retirement age. The strength of the rumor and its evocation of an official denial suggested that the end of the steel crisis was near. Indeed when their meeting at the Carlyle broke up at 5:10 P.M., Goldberg and Clifford knew that U.S. Steel would throw in the towel, but they were still unclear as to which of the possible rationalizations the company would employ in its public explanation.

At 5:28 P.M. the news arrived at the White House. Mrs. Barbara Gamarekian, a secretary in the White House press office, was checking the Associated Press news-ticker when suddenly the announcement appeared. U.S. Steel had rescinded its price increase. Mrs. Gamarekian ripped off the newstape and rushed unceremoniously into the office of Sorensen, who was on the phone talking with Acting Press Secretary Hatcher, now with the President in Norfolk, Virginia. "Well," Sorensen was saying, "I guess there isn't anything new." Mrs. Gamarekian laid the tape before him. "Wait a minute!" cried Sorensen. When the President emerged from the nuclear submarine Thomas A. Edison in Norfolk, Hatcher gave him the big news. Both sides in the dispute issued the inevitable public statements. U.S. Steel's President Worthington, in explaining his company's rescission of the entire 3.5 per cent price increase, explained that this latest price decision "was made in the light of the competitive developments today, and all other current circumstances including the removal of a serious obstacle to proper relations between Government and business." The "serious obstacle" was apparently the friction the steel dispute had generated between Washington and the steel price-raisers. In Norfolk, President Kennedy quickly issued a statement mild and conciliatory in tone.

> The people of the United States are most gratified by the announcements of Bethlehem and United States Steel Company that their proposed price increases are being rescinded. In taking the action at this time, they are serving the public interest and their actions will assist our common objective of strengthening our country and our economy.

The happenings of the rest of the day were anticlimactic. At 9:00 P.M. the parade of steel companies marching behind Bethlehem's and U.S. Steel's lead began. A spokesman for Youngstown Sheet and Tube announced that his company was canceling its price increase. One after another, the major steel companies made similar announcements. At the White House, where the atmosphere in the seventy-two-hour steel crisis had reached an intensity reminiscent of the 1960 electoral campaign, a relaxed interlude of exultation and post-mortem analysis was setting in. On the White House grounds a guard, upon learning of the victory over steel, exclaimed, "This'll get Kennedy reelected!"

Aftermath

Not all the forces started by the steel crisis were subsiding into quiescence. Senator Estes Kefauver announced that his Antitrust Subcommittee would subpoena the major steel companies for cost figures in a few days. The price-rise cancellations, a Kefauver aide stressed, would not change the subcommittee's plans. In contrast, Congressman Emanuel Celler, chairman of the House Antitrust Subcommittee, disclosed that an investigation scheduled for early May would not be made. "The penitent shall not be punished," he explained.

Attorney General Robert Kennedy was less conciliatory. The Justice Department's plans for the grand-jury investigation, he said, were unchanged. Another Justice Department official explained that the investigation would not be used as a club to bring prices down further, but would endeavor to discover whether there was a conspiracy in the quick succession of price rises following U.S. Steel's. A further question awaiting exploration was whether U.S. Steel was so strong that it constituted a monopoly under the Antitrust Laws.

Two Kennedys, Two Moods

While Robert Kennedy was moving sternly upon the several steel companies, his brother, the President, was waving a handful of olive branches to create an altogether opposite atmosphere of conciliation and good will. The President said at his press conference on April 19,

> First, let me make it clear that this Administration harbors no ill will against any individual, any industry, corporation or segment of the American economy. Our goals of economic growth and price stability are dependent upon the success of both corporations, business and labor and there can be no room on either side in this country at this time for any feelings of hostility or vindictiveness. When a mistake has been retracted and the public interest preserved, nothing is to be gained from further public recriminations.

The President concluded his prepared statement with an amiable comment about the current year's profits for industry in general and steel in particular. "And it is a fact," he added, "that the last quarter of last year and I think the first quarter of this year will be the highest profits in the history of this country . . . ."

In his answers to reporters' questions, the President continued to wave the olive branch at every opportunity.

> Q: . . . How does the change in the situation between last week and this affect the grand jury investigation . . . ?
>
> A: Well, the grand jury has been called in order to investigate a possible violation of the law, and this [is] a matter now before the grand jury, and, of course, in accordance with the procedures provided, this matter will be [followed through] to see if such a violation exists.
>
> Q: . . . *The Wall Street Journal* and some other spokesmen of business have accused you directly of having set the price in steel.
>
> A: . . . What we attempted to do was project before the steel companies the public interest and it was a combination of the public interest placed upon the table in front of them and competition which I think brought the price down by the fact that several companies refused to increase prices and therefore competition worked its will.
>
> Q: . . . Chairman Miller [Congressman William E. Miller, Republican National Chairman] and other Republicans have spoken with a good deal of criticism on the nocturnal activities of the Federal Bureau of Investigation. Could you shed any light on that, sir?
>
> A: . . . Reporters have called up a good many people in the middle of the night themselves . . . all we were attempting to do was to find out so that we could decide about the grand jury meeting . . . . Now both the reporters were very cooperative. I didn't realize they would be woken up at the time they were. The decision was made at an earlier time in the evening and I suppose making the connection, the F.B.I. followed ahead . . . .

This was by no means the only occasion on which President Kennedy worked to quench the flames of strife. At a news conference on May 9, he took up the task of softening his father's earthy allusion to businessmen that had seemed so apropos to Kennedy in the early hours of the price episode. Spurred by a reporter's question, the President said that his father's statement did not apply "to all businessmen" as had been reported "in one daily paper." It could not, commented Kennedy, because his father was a businessman himself. The President explained,

> He was critical of the steel men, and he worked for a steel company himself, and he was involved when he was a member of the Roosevelt Administration in the 1937 strike, and he formed an opinion which he imparted to me, and which I found appropriate that evening. But he confined it, and I would confine it . . . .

Reaffirming that "these generalizations are inaccurate and unfair," the President concluded by saying, "I felt at that time that we had not been treated altogether with frankness, and therefore I thought that his view had merit. But that is past. Now we are working together, I hope."

Not every sound heard after the steel dispute's termination echoed the President's tones of gentle magnanimity. There were several discords, many struck by major Republican personalities. In a television interview, Governor Nelson Rockefeller of New York said he considered the rescission of the steel price increase and President Kennedy's campaign to obtain it "a very sad proposition." What in particular was "sad"? "The way it developed, the timing, the reaction, the methods that were used," the Governor replied. "The methods on both sides?" he was asked. The Governor nodded his agreement.

Senate-House Republican leadership expressed its displeasure more emphatically. The fault, it said, lay entirely with the President. His confrontation of the steel industry, the Republican leadership charged in a lengthy statement, constituted "a display of naked political power never seen before in this nation." He had "directed or supported a series of governmental actions that imperiled basic American rights, went far beyond the law and were more characteristic of a police state than a free government." The statement, interestingly, did *not* defend the steel price increase, an omission which the Senate-House Democratic leaders seized upon in their rebuttal.

Rumblings of displeasure were also heard from the upper echelons of the business world. H. Ladd Plumley of Worcester, Massachusetts, president-elect of the U.S. Chamber of Commerce, noted that the government's many "pressure forces" in the dispute were having "an increasingly disquieting effect" on businessmen and investors. President Kennedy's assurances were a partial restorative, said Mr. Plumley, but his future actions would count more, and businessmen would be watching them closely.

The steel industry's principal trade magazines were appropriately sympathetic to the steel companies and condemnatory of President Kennedy.

"When the White House beat Big Steel to its knees," read an editorial in *Iron Age,* "it used pressure in pounds of steel pipe. This was applied sharply and quickly. Like rabbit punches." *Steel, The Metal Working Weekly,* termed the President's action "illogical and unbecoming to a chief of state," and its indication "that we are galloping down the road toward totalitarianism gave management just cause for apprehension."

U.S. Steel Is Indicted

President Kennedy's optimism about steel profits received partial but by no means complete fulfillment in the keenly awaited quarterly statement of U.S. Steel, made public on April 25. For the first quarter of 1962, the corporation made a profit of \$55,808,436, a return of 5.7 per cent on sales of \$978,219,633. The company declared its usual dividend of 75 cents a share. This 1962 profit figure was larger than the 4.5 per cent on sales in the depressed 1961 period but much smaller than that for the comparable 1960 period. Its 1962 financial situation, after the payment of dividends, the company said, left it with "no margin for reinvestment in the business." Now, as in the price controversy, U.S. Steel argued that its profits were "inadequate" to generate funds to keep its facilities fully competitive. During a press conference held in conjunction with the appearance of the quarterly statement, Roger Blough, discoursing on his company's future, pointed out that one of the things that would most seriously affect the demand for steel was "business confidence."

Two days later, U.S. Steel and Bethlehem were indicted in New York City by a federal grand jury on April 27 on charges of violating the Antitrust Laws. Also indicted were the Erie Forge and Steel Corporation of Erie, Pennsylvania, and the Midvale-Heppenstall Company of Philadelphia, the Open Die Forging Institute, Inc., a trade association, and five steel executives, including Erb Gurney and Robert S. Barnes of Bethlehem.

The defendants were charged with conspiring in violation of Section 1 of the Sherman Act to rig bids on products made by open-die forging—a process that imparts exceptional strength to steel by hammering or pressing it into desired shapes. The Defense Department is a major purchaser of such steel, and those indicted account for about half its production. The Forging Institute, the government contended, served as a clearing-house for price agreements among the defendants. All customer requests for quotations on forgings worth more than \$500 were relayed to the Institute. The resulting price discussions, the government said, were conducted either by telephone or at meetings of the Institute. Whenever the subject arose at the meetings, the secretary, who ordinarily kept minutes, was excused. According to the government, U.S. Steel did not participate directly in the reporting system for price inquiries, but simply reported customer inquiries to Bethlehem, who in turn reported them to the Institute. Bethlehem was accused of acting as liaison between U.S. Steel and the other defendants in the formulation of price agreements. Conviction would mean up to a year in prison and a $50,000 fine for each defendant. The maximum penalty for a corporate defendant would be a $50,000 fine.

When news of the indictment broke, President Worthington of U.S. Steel said that the development came as a "considerable surprise" because the company's policy "has been and is to comply fully with the antitrust laws." The company's employees, Worthington added, "know without question that they have no authority to enter into agreements with competitors which in any way restrict competition or restrain absolute freedom of action with respect to commercial matters." Heavy forgings, Worthington pointed out, "constitute . . . only about one-quarter of 1 per cent of its total sales. . . ." Bethlehem made a similar defense.

A statement from the Justice Department stressed that the indictment had no connection with the recent steel-price controversy, but grew out of an unrelated investigation begun more than a year ago. While finding this explanation plausible, the New York *Times* considered the timing of the indictment against Bethlehem and U.S. Steel "unfortunate." "It is bound to revive many of the fears and animosities," said the *Times,* "stirred by the recent battle over steel prices."

A Government-Industry Dialogue

During late April and early May, the steel situation, its past and future, became the focus for a "dialogue" between industry and government spokesmen. On April 27, E. J. Hanley, president of Allegheny Ludlum Steel, reflected on the recent price encounter. "The price of steel," he observed, "is set in the market place, where steel is in competition with aluminum, plastics, masonry, treated woods, glass, reinforced concrete, and many other alternative products, to say nothing of foreign-made steel." His company, said Hanley, did not raise prices because "in our judgment, our customers would not pay higher prices." "Old fashioned economics," or the economics of the market place, he contended, should have been given a chance to operate on the attempted price increase without government intervention.

On April 30, President Kennedy addressed the fiftieth annual meeting of the U.S. Chamber of Commerce in Washington. The speech was conciliatory and carefully directed to allay business fears of sweeping governmental intervention in private pricing policies. "We have many burdens in Washington," said the President. "We do not want the added burden of determining individual prices for individual products." Rather, prices had to be set by private decision and it was up to business to follow "responsible" pricing practices. The President did not specify what kinds of action the government would consider "responsible" or what would happen in the face of irresponsibility. He said merely, "These areas where conflict exists between what I would call private interests and the general welfare must be met, and it seems to me by assumption of responsibility by all of us who care for our country."

In his preview of future government-business relations, the President took pains to declare that all subsequent union demands for wage increases would be viewed critically and that every effort would be made to create "a climate of collective bargaining in which increased wages are held within the appropriate limits of rising productivity, a rising productivity that will also provide for investments in modernization, for profits, and even we hope lower prices, to stimulate increased purchasing." The President also alluded to the bill to provide an 8 per cent tax credit for new investment that was before Congress and promised to order depreciation liberalizations in the tax laws just as large as the federal budget could stand. Modernized plants and stable prices, he predicted, would win ever larger foreign markets for American business.

In the weeks that followed, the President circumspectly followed a course of moderation in his relations with business, bidding for its cooperation and minimizing his powers. Clearly the President wished to avoid above all else uniting the business community against his Administration. In a speech at Yale University on June 11, Kennedy called for cooperation between government and business in pumping new life into the nation's economy. On the same day at the White House he discussed with business leaders the problem of the balance of payments and the outflow of gold. A participant in the discussion was Roger Blough. In July, the President engaged in an exchange of letters with David Rockefeller, president of the Chase Manhattan Bank, on the question "What to do about the economy." The letters, constructive in tone and remarkable for their wide area of agreement, were published in *Life* magazine. "What I am concerned about," the President declared in September to the White House Conference of Business Magazine Editors and Publishers concerning Administration-business relations, "is that we have as close an understanding as possible."

On May 7, U.S. Steel had a major opportunity to offer its own reflections on recent happenings and its vision of the future. The occasion was the annual stockholders' meeting in the blue-draped field house of the Stevens Institute of Technology in Hoboken, New Jersey. Some 1,300 stockholders were on hand eagerly awaiting the report of Board Chairman Blough.

Blough began his report, fittingly titled "In the Public Interest," with the observation, "It has been sort of a warm spring." The stockholders applauded. They applauded again when he declared, "I do not believe that the public interest can ever be served by hostility between Government and business." Reading in a quiet manner, Blough cited the familiar arguments about steel's profit squeeze to demonstrate that the steel price rise had been made "in the public interest and in the interests of all concerned with maintaining a profitable and competitive enterprise." He pointed out that U.S. Steel had received no assurance that the other steel producers would follow its pricing lead, and, in fact, when Bethlehem Steel led the trail down-hill by rescinding, "Since all companies in a buyers' market must necessarily meet the lower price of their competition, United States Steel had no recourse but to do the same. . . ." Blough tossed back one of Kennedy's olive branches when he added, "We hoped that our action would help to remove what had clearly become a serious obstacle to the maintenance of a proper relationship between government and the business community."

However, Blough remained upset over "two vital areas of misunderstanding." The first was the belief that "there is something special—something economically inhibitory—about the price of steel." Milk and bread prices had risen about 5 and 10 per cent respectively since 1958, and the cost of the federal government as seen in its budget had risen 24 per cent, while steel sought only a 3.5 per cent rise over its 1958 level. Blough rejected the idea that such a rise constituted "an intolerable threat to the security and economic welfare of this nation" as well as the belief that "Government can ever serve the national interest in peacetime by seeking to control prices. . . ."

The second area of misunderstanding stemmed from the nation's lack of appreciation for the relative stagnation of corporate profits in the past ten to twelve years. Blough cited U.S. Department of Commerce data showing that while employee compensation had nearly doubled from 1950 to 1961, and while business taxes had risen 70 per cent, "corporate profits had gone up by only 2 per cent. . . ." Blough argued that this deterioration in our national profit position was "weakening our industrial potential" and preventing a maximum rate of growth by allowing the retention of "some 90 billions of dollars worth" of obsolete industrial plant and equipment. Blough was heartened, however, by Kennedy's statement that "a fair profit" was the key to economic growth, modernization of plant facilities, and increased productivity.

Blough was given a standing ovation for his report. In the tumultuous discussion period that followed, one stockholder suggested that Blough run for United States President and another that he resign. Said a critic, "I wonder if it isn't just as imperative for some of the officers of United States Steel to modernize their minds as it is for the corporation to modernize its facilities?" As the session drew to a close, a lady stockholder thanked Mr. Blough "for the humiliation with which he has conducted the meeting." Amid the laughter, other stockholders explained to each other, "She means humility."

Why Did U.S. Steel Do It?

Roger Blough's explanation at the stockholders' meeting of why U.S. Steel had raised its prices did not altogether satisfy his fellow executives in the industry. Wherever they gathered, two questions set them buzzing: Why did U.S. Steel raise its prices when it did? And why was its timing so bad?

U.S. Steel's own Commercial Department was very doubtful about whether the price increase could be made to stand. The mystery deepened when it became known that prior to U.S. Steel's action, Bethlehem Steel had considered taking the step but had decided against it. Why had U.S. Steel stepped in where its fellow giant had feared to tread?

U.S. Steel's strategy seems to have been based in part on the assumption that other companies would follow its lead because they were in comparably adverse circumstances. For decades, as discussed earlier, U.S. Steel had taken the lead in setting prices that others followed. It proposed to do so in 1962, although its leadership was more susceptible to challenge, owing to the decline of its relative position vis-à-vis other steel companies. Another factor in U.S. Steel's calculations seemed to be the possibility that if another company took the lead, it might raise prices on a selective basis, rather than across the board. In U.S. Steel's judgment, only the latter was suitable for its needs. It chose to lead the industry not from strength, as in bygone days, but from weakness.

To some, U.S. Steel's behavior is largely explained by its excessive introversion as a corporation, its long-standing insensitivity to market pressures. The signals, all too glaringly visible in the market place, warned of the folly of a price increase. Demand was soft, orders were declining, and 40 per cent of mill capacity lay idle. Foreign competition was rising, spurred by highly efficient new mills enjoying increasing capacity. The displacement of steel by competitive materials like aluminum, plastics, and concrete was accelerating. According to the general industry view, it was no time for a price rise. In the face of market outlook and informed opinion, Roger Blough remained unimpressed. There was nothing particularly wrong with the April timing, he has always maintained. There is no such thing as a good time for a price rise. And, in fact, one advantage to this timing, some have said, was that it would allow officials of the corporation to raise prices before they announced their first-quarter earnings for 1962; dividend payments were barely being met, and they feared that revealing earnings figures might cause a drop in the value of U.S. Steel stock.

Blue Monday

The economic circumstances of the steel industry, particularly of its biggest members, evidenced no improvement in the immediate aftermath of the price crisis. If anything, conditions seemed worse. Steel-producers envisioned themselves as entering a profit-pinching period ahead. The attempted price rise had failed. On July 1, the new labor contract would go into effect, involving a 2.5 per cent rise in labor costs, by industry calculations. The signing of the new labor contract in April, some three months before its effective date, had snuffed out at an earlier stage than usual the buildup of inventories by steel-users in anticipation of a strike.

Clearly, there would be no strike, and promptly after the new contract was signed, steel orders fell. Within three weeks Bethlehem Steel's order backlog fell about 21 per cent. At U.S. Steel, Chairman Blough was predicting a decline in second-quarter shipments.

Steel was not the only commodity in the American economy suffering decline. In the weeks following the termination of the steel-price crisis, the stock market had been steadily falling. So pronounced was the drop that the term "Kennedy Bear Market" was enjoying ever wider usage. Speculation concerning the cause of the phenomenon was becoming a growing preoccupation. One market analyst, Lawrence Fertig, contended that when Kennedy quashed the steel-price rise, he was asserting in effect that profits were ample in steel and in industry generally, and, "when investors realized that the President would act in accordance with these erroneous ideas they sold stocks because the prospect for profits seemed dim." (Later research, such as a 1963 SEC study, rejected the view that Kennedy's steel action started the stock slide.)

The bear market—Kennedy's or otherwise—plunged to its bottommost depths on May 28, a day that will be dolefully remembered as "Blue Monday." On that day, shares on the New York Stock Exchange fell 20.8 billion dollars in value in the longest one-day drop since the horrendous "Black Tuesday" in 1929. On May 28, 1,212 issues fell, the largest ever in a single day. IBM plummeted 37.5 points. A.T. & T. fell 11 points, Standard Oil of New Jersey 5, and Du Pont 12.5. U.S. Steel dropped 1.9 points, Bethlehem Steel 2.5, and Inland Steel .5. The declining steel stocks were accompanied by an announcement from the American Iron and Steel Institute that steel production was down for the eighth successive week since the signing of the new labor-industry contract. For the first time in more than a year, steel tonnage was below 60 per cent of capacity. Indeed the figure for the previous week had been 57 per cent. Some big mills had orders on their books for only 50 per cent of capacity and predictors estimated that before many weeks less than 50 per cent of the industry's capacity would be employed. Readers of *Iron Age* could recall its April 19 editorial on the steel price rescission, closing with what now seemed an all too prophetic question: "In a most spectacular pyrotechnical display of power the President won. Or did he?"

The day after Blue Monday, the stock market made a strong recovery, wiping out 60 per cent of the losses. But in the weeks that followed, the market continued far below a former lofty plateau that had been considered "unrealistically high" in the opinion of many, and the industry-wide steel data showed not a flutter of improvement. *Fortune* magazine reported in July,

> The President asks visitors what it is that business men want him to do or say beyond the conciliatory and encouraging statements he feels he has already made. They want to hear him make it clear that he understands

what business confidence really is . . . to make it unequivocally clear that he has no intention in the future of trying to fix prices. This, of course, might be taken as a tacit admission that he had been mistaken in trying to fix steel prices, and it is a rule among politicians never to admit that they ever made a mistake. . . . Business men, in short, would like to hear him say he understands that they are in business to make a profit.

The Steel Crisis in Perspective

A Developing Historiography

The steel crisis was not long over before the principal participants, with an eye on history, took pains to provide vindications of their conduct.

In an article in *Look* magazine on January 29, 1963, Roger Blough denied that he had "purposely lulled President Kennedy into the false impression that U.S. Steel would not raise prices, and then raised them." Blough also stated that his meeting with Kennedy on April 10 was not "a calculated affront" but a courteous gesture to inform the President of the price increase before its public announcement. Probably the most interesting part of the article is its analysis of Kennedy's behavior. Blough wrote,

> I believe that at least part of President Kennedy's vehement public reaction to the news of steel's price increase was not really because he expected a nationwide inflationary spiral to result from it, but because he had been hoping for a steel-price status quo for reasons involving his relations with labor. His earlier stand against a 35-hour work week had displeased the labor unions. I believe that he and Secretary Goldberg felt that an increase in steel prices, following the early wage negotiations, would be viewed as evidence that the Administration's policies were adverse to labor's interests.

President Kennedy, for his part, engaged in a post-mortem analysis of the steel events in the course of a lengthy televised interview with William Lawrence, George Herman, and Sander Vanocur on December 16, 1962. "Some people have suggested that in retrospect perhaps you would not have acted so vigorously. Is there any truth in this suggestion?" the President was asked.

The President answered as follows:

> I must say it would have been a very serious situation; though I don't like to rake over old fires, I think it would have been a serious situation if I had not attempted with all my influence to try to get a rollback, because there was an issue of good faith involved. The steel union had accepted the most limited settlement that they had had since the end of the second war; they had accepted it three or four months ahead; they did it in part, I think, because I said that we could not afford another inflationary spiral, that it would affect our competitive position abroad, so

Rising Controversy over the 1962 Steel-Pricing Dispute:

1. U. S. Steel's price rise was seen by supporters as legitimate free enterprise, by critics as profiteering.

Holland in the Chicago *Tribune*

Herblock in *The Washington Post*

2. Steel partisans viewed Kennedy's reaction as inappropriate to the provocation and as overly authoritarian.

Lou Grant in the St. Paul *Pioneer Press*

Fischetti in the New York *Herald Tribune*

3. Kennedy's image varied: to some he was an American hero; to others he was a figure drawing on the New Deal anti-business tradition.

Mauldin in the St. Louis *Post-Dispatch*

Bob Taylor in the Dallas *Times Herald*

4. In the afterglow, observers remained split: some saw industry maintaining its arrogant course; others saw its confidence seriously shaken.

"Very well, then....IT'S WAR!"

nterlandi in the Des Moines *Register*

Kennedy Did It With His Little Blow-Torch

Knox in the Nashville *Banner*

they signed up. Then when their last contract was signed, which was the Friday or Saturday before, then steel put its prices up immediately. It seemed to me that the question of good faith was involved, and that if I had not attempted, after asking the unions to accept the non-inflationary settlement, . . . to use my influence to have the companies hold their prices stable, I think the union could have rightfully felt that they had been misled. In my opinion it would have endangered the whole bargaining between labor and management, would have made it impossible for us to exert any influence from the public point of view in the future on these great labor-management disputes which do affect the public interest. So I have no regrets. The fact is, we were successful.

Now, supposing we had tried and made a speech about it and then failed. I would have thought that would have been an awful setback to the office of the Presidency. Now, I just think, looking back on it, that I would not change it at all. There is no sense in raising hell and then not being successful. There is no sense in putting the office of the Presidency on the line on an issue and then being defeated. Now, an unfortunate repercussion of that was the strong feeling that the government might interfere in a good many labor-management matters, or that it might interfere in the whole question of the free enterprise system. It was regrettable that that general conclusion was drawn in this particular incident. Given the problem that I had on that Tuesday night, I must say I think we had to do everything we could to get it reversed.

Kennedy's View of the Presidency

The televised interview in which Kennedy commented on the steel crisis was also the occasion of a remarkably wide-ranging discussion of the Presidency itself. Rarely has a President talked about his office with such candor and with so many rewarding flashes of revelation. Kennedy's remarks illuminate both his method in crises like steel and his approach to the general functioning of the office.

> LAWRENCE: . . . Has your experience in the office matched your expectations? . . .
>
> KENNEDY: Well, I think in the first place the problems are more difficult than I had imagined they were. Secondly, there is a limitation upon the ability of the United States to solve these problems. . . . The responsibilities placed on the United States are greater than I imagined them to be, and there are greater limitations upon our ability to bring about a favorable result than I had imagined . . . .
>
> LAWRENCE: . . . How does a President go about making a decision, like Cuba, for example?
>
> KENNEDY: The most recent one was hammered out . . . on policy and decision over a period of five or six days. During that period, the 15 people more or less who were directly consulted frequently changed their view, because whatever action we took had so many disadvantages to it . . . Finally, however, I think a general consensus developed, and [it] certainly seemed, after all alternatives were examined, that the course

of action that we finally adopted was the right one. . . . it is very difficult to always make judgments here about what the effect will be of our decisions on other countries. In this case [Cuba, 1962], it seems to me that we did pick the right one; in Cuba of 1961 we picked the wrong one.

HERMAN: . . . You have said and the Constitution says that the decision can be made only by the President.

KENNEDY: . . . President Eisenhower said to me on January 19 . . . "There are no easy matters that will ever come to you as President. If they are easy, they will be settled at a lower level." . . . So this contributes to some of the burdens of the office of the Presidency, which other Presidents have commented on.

VANOCUR: . . . During the Cuban crisis, there was some problem . . . about the possibility of a President talking in very private and secret conversations with his advisors, and that somehow leaking out. Do you think that this is going to inhibit the free, frank flow of advice that every President has to have?

KENNEDY: No . . . I said at the time of the Cuban disaster in April of 1961 that success has a hundred fathers and defeat is an orphan. I suppose when something goes well, there is more tendency to talk at all levels, and frequently the reports are inaccurate. I would say the security is pretty good at the National Security Council. It is unfortunate when it is breached.

VANOCUR: Is it true that during your first year, sir, you would get on the phone personally to the State Department and try to get a response to some inquiry that had been made?

KENNEDY: Yes, I still do that when I can, because I think there is a great tendency in government to have papers stay on desks too long . . . After all, the President can't administer a department, but at least he can be a stimulant.

VANOCUR: . . . You once said that you were reading more and enjoying it less. Are you still as avid a newspaper reader? . . .

KENNEDY: Oh, yes. . . . there is a terrific disadvantage not having the abrasive quality of the press applied to you daily, to an administration, even though we never like it, and even though we wish they didn't write it, and even though we disapprove, there isn't any doubt that we could not do the job at all in a free society without a very, very active press. . . .

And on the subject of patronage, the President added:

. . . That is not the power of the Presidency, patronage, at all. They are filled in the first months. Most of those jobs belong to the members of the Congress, anyway. So patronage is not a factor. . . .

A Further Perspective: Democratic Presidents and the Business Community

The steel case, it should be noted, is by no means typical of Kennedy's approach to the business community. In actuality, his relations with business have been less acrimonious than those of his two most recent Democratic predecessors, Franklin D. Roosevelt and Harry S. Truman.

Roosevelt was constantly at loggerheads with business. His New Deal, a program of extensive economic regulation and reform, encountered bitter business resistance. Businessmen contested every piece of New Deal legislation in the courts, often successfully. Roosevelt became a widely hated symbol in the business community, and he responded at times with severe attacks upon "unscrupulous money-changers" and "economic royalists." Needless to say, few businessmen occupied posts in his Administration.

Although Harry Truman was briefly a businessman as coproprietor of a haberdashery, he fared little better than Roosevelt with the business community. His Fair Deal, an extension of New Deal economic and social policies, helped make the phrase "welfare state" a part of American usage. This hardly won him friends among businessmen. Neither did his advocacy of price and rent control, his close ties with labor leaders, and his occasional condemnation of certain business groups such as "the real estate lobby" as a "little group of ruthless men."

Aside from the steel dispute, Kennedy's treatment of business has been studiously conciliatory. Far less friction with business has existed during his Administration than during Truman's or Roosevelt's. Kennedy, as a possessor of wealth accumulated by his father in a classic business career, has personally enjoyed greater acceptance in the business community than his predecessors. Many more businessmen have been appointed to key posts in Kennedy's Administration than in Roosevelt's or Truman's. Moderation has typified Kennedy's economic policies. His Council of Economic Advisers, for example, is steadily more conservative than that body was under the chairmanship of Leon Keyserling in the Truman Administration. Significantly, Keyserling in 1962 was as persistent and forceful a critic of Kennedy's CEA as any businessman.

Continuing Crisis: A Condition of the Presidency

The President lives with problems that are never solved. Although sometimes key problems are reduced to temporary quiescence, all too often they flare up again with unexpected force. Even the most skillful crisis management cannot do the work of solid policy-making. Crisis action detached from long-range legislative policies may bring only short-range victory. In many instances, the aftermath of vigorous Presidential action has nullified part of the apparent victory. For instance, in the fall of 1962, President Kennedy prevailed on the Soviet Union to remove missiles, missile sites, and a few thousand Soviet military technicians from Cuba. In 1963, however, the Cuban question remained hotly controversial and a source of substantial criticism leveled at the Administration by Republicans such as Senator Kenneth Keating (New York). President Kennedy, likewise, saw the successful enrollment of Negro student James Meredith in the University of Mississippi in the fall of 1962 through Presidential support become a continuing problem of enforcement and even potential disaster. Formidable local harassments almost forced Meredith to withdraw from the school and undoubtedly discouraged other Negro applicants. In the same way, the President was able to apply highly dramatic pressures to the steel companies during the steel crisis. However, when this period of crisis passed, steel prices reverted to the ultimate control of private corporations.

In periods of national emergency, the government has been able to intrude effectively on economic questions like price determination. Thus during World War II, government price controls were instituted and administered through Congressional legislation. But in non-emergency periods, government influence on economic decisions is usually limited to indirect pressures. Each President must try to create a business climate favorable to his Administration's concept of the national interest. A President can do this, for example, by prevailing on Congress to pass legislation that makes certain types of investment more profitable. Thus President Kennedy may encourage plant modernization and strengthen the position of domestic mills in the world steel market by manipulating tax and depreciation policies. But the key decisions—the allocation of funds to investment, profits, and plowback into renovation—remain with the steel industry itself. The President can coax, influence, and persuade. But he cannot dictate these decisions.

And as it turned out, President Kennedy was able to stem the steel price increase for only a relatively short time. Almost a year to the day after his challenge of the steel price rise in 1962, Kennedy was confronted by a new and more skillfully launched effort by the steel companies to raise prices on various steel products. Wheeling Steel Corporation was the first company that broke the price line when it put forth its proposal for selective price increases on April 9, 1963. The company's announcement was received by several days of careful silence and internal debate at the White House. The President was faced with several alternatives: attempting a new "hold-the-line" intervention, accepting the price rises without protest, or adopting the view that the new situation was different. The President's prestige and good faith were not now involved as in 1962. Kennedy chose the last of these possibilities when he said on April 11, 1963, that "selected price adjustments up or down, as prompted by changes in supply or demand," need not upset over-all price stability.

The other steel companies interpreted this statement as a green light for price increases. One by one the major companies announced price increases. The Administration took no countermeasures.

Conflicting Interpretations of the Kennedy Strategy

The Misuse of Governmental Power: A Conservative Critique

In the eyes of the business community and those who articulated its views, Kennedy in the steel dispute had used his power illegitimately. Neither the Constitution nor any statute, in this view, empowered him to set steel prices. The determination of prices, as Roger Blough and other businessmen saw it, was a cardinal decision that was the exclusive prerogative of private enterprise. Presidential intervention in Kennedy's fashion involved nothing less than the substitution of a managed for a free economy.

Even worse, in what might be termed the conservative view, the President had resorted to a variety of expedients that were wholly alien to the role of government in a free society. The use of police, the bringing of legal actions to coerce the steel companies, the juggling of defense contracts were repugnant to the American political tradition. The business community was further disturbed by the fact that the Administration by no means confided its use of "muscular" tactics to the steel episode but applied them to other situations as well in 1962.

One such episode involved paying ransom to Fidel Castro in the form of baby foods, drugs, and hospital and medical equipment to bring the release of prisoners captured in the abortive Bay of Pigs invasion in 1961. Officially, the Administration had played no part in amassing the $53 million represented by the materials offered to Castro. "This," the President said, "is being done by a private committee." In actuality, the Justice Department, by various inducements, persuaded the drug and chemical companies to "donate" their products and railroads, truckers, airlines, and shipping firms to "donate" their services. Of the several inducements, the most powerful was one permitting drug, chemical, and food companies to write off $25 million of the $53 million ransom as "charitable" deductions. The generosity of this treatment contrasted sharply with the Administration's general policy of closely scrutinizing all charitable deductions by the taxpayer.

The Activist President: Liberal Defenses of the Strong Presidency

On the other hand, this case study is seen by some, particularly by liberals, as a Presidential success story—an account of how John Kennedy got exactly what he wanted: the complete and unconditional revocation of U.S. Steel's price increase. If a job manual should ever be prepared some day for the guidance of American Presidents, chances are that the chapter entitled "How to Succeed in Crisis by Really Trying" will portray Kennedy's encounter with steel as a model to be copied and admired. His victory over "the Steel Duke" (as the popular recording "The First Family" called Roger Blough) will long be remembered.

Kennedy's victory over steel improved his standing in the community of liberal Democrats. For some time, this group had been chafing under the Administration's seemingly soft approach in social legislation. The tendency of "the New Frontier" to represent little more than a catch phrase and the President's seeming reserve toward liberals had brought the quality of his liberalism into serious question. In confronting Big Steel, Kennedy delighted many liberals with his courage and fight, proving that he was not, as they had feared, merely chilly and dispassionate.

Kennedy, in this liberal view, has a crisis style. Crisis is conflict, actual or threatened, and Kennedy and his colleagues bring to it qualities that count: shrewdness in strategy, sharpness at maneuver, and a zest for conflict with the President himself in the thick of it. The steel episode leaves no doubt that Kennedy's course is in accord with Robert Frost's counsel, offered during Inaugural Week, that the new Chief Executive should be more Irish than Harvard in his approach to Presidential power. In his counterthrust at U.S. Steel, Kennedy seemed to bring every kind of pressure into the fight except the United States Marines. Presidential prestige was pitted against U.S. Steel's power; the Presidential news conference rallied popular opinion and focused the spotlight of opprobrium on Roger Blough. Robert Kennedy unloosed the Justice Department's massive law-enforcement apparatus on the company. The "money pressure" was also turned on when the Defense Department announced that its multimillion-dollar contracts would be allocated to those steel companies that went along with the Administration in lieu of those that resisted it. Simultaneously, the "friendly" telephone call went out to steel companies on the fence in their pricing decisions, with its implicit threat of punitive antitrust action and deprivation of governmental business and favors.

Liberal partisans would argue that the Kennedy Administration's crisis style was a work of political art. The lines of attack were nicely selected, balanced, and coordinated. Each actor deftly handled his assigned task— the President his press-conference speech; the CEA and Labor Department statisticians the preparation of the required data; Sorensen the bright rhetoric; and Goldberg and Clifford their dual diplomacy, one supplying the heavy candor, the other the "outsider's" friendly interest. Equally impressive was the Administration's alacrity in throwing together an *ad hoc* crisis work force drawn from several parts of the Executive Branch, unfettered by procedural red tape and able to act fast. In all of it, John F. Kennedy was both field commander and front-line soldier.

Part of the Administration's success lay in astutely perceiving that not all steel companies were alike, either in operating policies or in political outlook. Out of this observation, the "divide-and-conquer" strategy to exploit these intrinsic differences emerged. The Administration gave up as "lost" those older, conservative corporations with less efficient plant facilities (and therefore a lower rate of profit), estimating that they could be coped with only by naked force. But the Administration deemed "reachable" by subtle semicoercive persuasion the contrasting type of steel company, typified by Inland and Kaiser. These smaller, newer, and more efficient companies could afford to make profits at lower prices through increased volume at the expense of the higher-priced companies. And perhaps companies like Inland enjoyed a reputation for public-mindedness partly because they could better afford to comply with government purposes in the economic sphere. To these companies holding out against a price increase, the Executive Branch dangled the lure of privileged access to government goodwill and, more tangibly, to Defense Department contracts. In a further effort, Administration officials, including the President, showered key personnel in the holdout steel companies with phone calls, in which little was said but much was conveyed.

One considerable advantage of the Administration's approach to the steel-pricing crisis, Kennedy partisans would argue, was that it could win solely with means already at hand. Nothing had to be asked from Congress. No House Rules Committee had to be circumvented or outwitted. No Senate opposition leadership had to be blandished or neutralized. Kennedy was therefore spared from working with his weakest tools. Had a bill been initiated in Congress, an outcome in Kennedy's favor would have been extremely doubtful. The uncertainties that the legislative process holds for the President is well illustrated by Kennedy's own record of success and failure with the Eighty-Seventh Congress. According to figures in the *Congressional Quarterly*, Congress in Kennedy's first year of office (1961) approved 48.4 per cent of his legislative requests and in his second year (1962), 44.3 per cent of his requests. (The comparable figures for President Eisenhower's first two years of office are 72.7 per cent and 64.7 per cent.) Kennedy's principal victory in his two years of office, and probably the only one that deserved to be called major, was the Trade Expansion Act of 1962. His most obvious defeats were in the field of education, where only two of his twenty-two requests received enactment. Other important proposals lost were those for medical care for the aged, the establishment of a cabinet-level department of urban affairs, the barring of arbitrary use of literacy tests as qualifications for voting, the establishment of standby power to lower taxes, the withholding of taxes on dividend and interest income at the source, and the permanent strengthening of the unemployment-insurance system. The sheer number and variety of the President's defeats suggest all too clearly the formidable hazards awaiting Presidential enterprise in legislation.

In addition, exponents of this view would argue, avoiding legislative action indirectly helped the business community as well. The ideological conflict between Kennedy and Blough would surely have been more protracted and embittered if the introduction of legislation had pulled it into the halls of Congress. Moreover, activist partisans would point out, despite the stock-market crash in May 1962, the suppression of a steel price increase contributed to the favorable appearance of the over-all 1962 price index. The Consumer Price Index, as reported by the federal Bureau of Labor Statistics, rose only 1.2 per cent in the period from December 1961 to December 1962. Comparable figures for other recent years are 1.1 per cent for the 1960–61 period; 3.5 per cent for 1956–57; and 2.8 per cent for 1957–58. Even the stock market presented a more cheerful aspect at the end of 1962. Dow Jones averages reached levels close to those existing before the steel crisis.

Partisans of Kennedy as an active President would argue that his economic influence may still have been lingering in the steel community even in April 1963. Although all the major companies raised their prices, their method and style of doing so varied from that of 1962. President Kennedy announced at the time of the first steel company's price increase that *selective* price rises were not necessarily incompatible with price stability. And all the major companies thereafter announced increases that were selective rather than across the board (as in 1962). For example, U.S. Steel, one of the later companies to announce increases, raised prices on the smallest number of items (despite Roger Blough's contention during the 1962 dispute that selective price increases would not be sufficient to solve U.S. Steel's financial problems).

In 1963, the steel companies seem to have acted with an eye to the Department of Justice's reaction. Each company initially followed its own pattern on prices. Even for those products that most companies did raise prices on, such as cold-rolled sheet and strip steel, increases varied from $5 to $6.50 a ton. This made the price increase atypical in steel history, since the industry had usually followed the first (and largest) company in pricing.

Kennedy partisans would argue that it was the memory of Presidential wrath that prompted the companies to choose their course with such unusual care. The diversity of price increases and the tact with which they were announced kept open the possibility of Presidential response. At any rate, they would contend that perhaps even the more conservative steel companies took to heart the lesson in "Presidential economics" administered a year earlier.

The Prince *and the Presidency*

A third kind of appraisal stands between the extremes of approval and condemnation. This view stems from the Machiavellian tradition of *Realpolitik*. It evaluates success by judging the appropriateness of means to the end and by weighing the prices paid against the gains won. Readers of *The Prince* would probably rate Kennedy's action in the steel dispute as poor because he "overreacted" to the situation. That is, he applied more power than was necessary to force the steel companies to rescind their price increases. The President's response was based upon an overestimation of the companies' strength. In actuality, their economic condition was weak, characterized by a declining use of their production facilities, falling demand, and increasing foreign competition. These circumstances made the steel industry extremely vulnerable to any kind of Presidential pressure. But, in fact, one could note that a year later, in April 1963, when the steel industry was operating at nearly 80 per cent of capacity, the Administration made no attempt to deter the steel companies from introducing price increases on a selective basis. As noted above, the President's prestige was not involved in 1963 as in 1962. Furthermore, the steel companies were in a stronger economic position, and the products they were raising prices on were not those suffering heavy foreign competition.

To bring the companies to submission in 1962, Kennedy employed extreme weapons. The use of the FBI, the pressure of the defense contracts, the antitrust prosecutions totaled a kind of "overkill" to subdue the companies when they could conceivably have been brought into line by less dramatic means. In using power excessively, the President impaired the image of himself as a master of restraint in the conduct of his office, as a Chief Executive who regularly met crises with understated actions. Because of his overuse of power in the steel episode, Kennedy was establishing a rival image of a Chief Executive who, when driven to anger, would place no limits on the weapons used to bring the offender to terms.

Ironically, the pressures that the President applied to the steel companies, although sensational in appearance, would have been highly limited in short-range effect. The antitrust threat, despite its ominous sound, had the force of a pop-gun. The steel companies are seasoned survivors of antitrust litigation, in which they have been involved over the years. As the companies well knew, an antitrust suit would be a prolonged process of three or four years, and while it might have elements of unpleasantness and uncertainty, it would threaten no major alteration of industry organization and practice. Likewise, the Senatorial investigation was an old experience to the companies; although long on publicity, a strong conservative coalition would render it short on concrete result. The manipulation of defense contracts was also a highly limited expedient. Contract awards are governed by competitive bidding laws that would give even companies in the Administration's disfavor an opportunity to secure contracts.

Thus, this pragmatic type of appraisal would stress Kennedy's error in choosing a method of action in the steel crisis that lacked the actual potency of a frontal attack but still *appeared* to be just as threatening. The disadvantage of using such dramatic, public tactics to gain Presidential ends is that the tactic threatens to become ineffective (even dangerous) if used frequently. Kennedy was hampered in the 1963 price rise by the fact that he had acted so vigorously in 1962. The bad taste left by the "strong-arm" tactics of the Executive Branch took more than a year to wear off. For example, one of the actions most damaging to the public image of the Executive Branch was its authorization of the early morning FBI phone calls and visits to reporters who had been present for Bethlehem's President Martin's statement. The Administration later claimed that it had given instructions to interview the reporters much earlier in the evening. It is impossible to know whether the time lag was the result of a bureaucratic blunder or whether a time lag existed at all.

If Kennedy had correctly assessed his opponents' strength, he might have chosen a mode of action that minimized the less desirable effects on public opinion, on his prospective legislative program in Congress, and of course, on business confidence.

Kennedy received criticism for his action not only from conservative public opinion, but from liberals as well. Something of the disarray that Kennedy caused to his image is suggested by an article in the *New Republic* of April 30, 1962, by Charles A. Reich of the Yale Law School. The *New Republic* is a staunch liberal journal and Reich is a former law clerk and a warm admirer of Justice Hugo Black. Reich objected to the atmosphere of "intimidation" and to the "irresponsibility" involved in the Administration's method. When steel prices rose, the Administration's prosecutorial zeal also rose. When steel prices were lowered, Administration pressures subsided on all fronts. "Are crimes by steel and other companies permitted so long as the criminals 'cooperate' with the Administration?" asked Reich. Other businesses that depend more than steel does upon government and popular approval would presumably be even more susceptible to Presidential coercion. Much of what the Administration accomplished by open pressure in the steel dispute might be done hereafter merely by subtle suggestion, suggested Reich.

The second cost of the steel dispute was its somewhat harmful effect upon Kennedy's legislative relations. The extent to which the dispute increased his difficulties in getting legislation through Congress cannot be measured, but it has provided a symbol for rallying the President's opposition, which paints him as an excessively power-oriented Chief Executive. "The Kennedys," Congressman John Lindsay (Republican of New York) said on one occasion, "have made basic grabs for power that are offensive to conservatives and liberals alike." Yet, for all that, the steel dispute did not prevent the implementation of the important 1962 Foreign Trade Act, giving the President new powers.

The third price was paid by Kennedy in business confidence. Although much research holds otherwise, considerable business opinion developed that the stock-market crash was caused by the business community's recoil from Kennedy's handling of the steel dispute. The market decline was a serious risk the President had to contemplate in deciding to move vigorously against U.S. Steel. After his triumph, he had to work hard to convince business that he was not about to launch a concerted attack on its interests.

Conciliation was his watchword to business. It was good economics, and therefore good politics, for Kennedy to be "nice" to business once the crisis was past.

In retrospect, to students of American Government, the steel-pricing crisis may become a celebrated example of the impact of Presidential politics on domestic economics. Each side seems to have learned significant lessons. To the President, the lesson of the cumulative effect of power, the costs of "overkill," seemed especially clear. The steel industry, and other American businesses, learned the high costs of affronting Presidential dignity and the high costs of bad timing. To both President and steel industry there was the continuing lesson of Blue Monday, that American government and American industry cannot wrangle in public with impunity.

2

CONGRESS

Schools, Scholarships, and Congressmen

The Kennedy Aid-to-Education Program

Conclusions : pg.96-105

Hugh Douglas Price

AMERICANS over the age of ten generally regard education as "a good thing." Aside from its intrinsic values, it increases the earning power of the individual, promotes the economic growth of the community, and strengthens the defense potential of the nation. Further, in a democratic country a certain level of popular education is necessary. It is no surprise that American politicians are as agreed on the virtues of education as they are on those of motherhood. The question of whether federal aid for schools is "a good thing" is, however, quite another matter.

This is an account of how Congress responded to President Kennedy's proposals for federal aid to education. It was just one month after his inauguration that the President sent to Congress his 1961 Message on Education. In it he asked for: (1) a $2.3 billion three-year program of federal aid for public schools for construction and aid for teacher salaries, (2) a $1.5 billion five-year program of low-interest federal loans for the construction of college classrooms and other academic facilities, and (3) an $892 million five-year program of 212,500 undergraduate scholarships providing up to $1,000 per year to talented young persons in need of financial assistance to obtain their education.

By 1963 the President had been defeated on all three proposals, as well as on some additional education requests.

Shortly after the Supreme Court held that an official school prayer was unconstitutional, the President quipped at the 1963 annual Gridiron Club dinner, "My school bill is very constitutional. It hasn't got a prayer." His audience, the elite of Washington journalism, was delighted by the Presidential pun. Moreover, the journalists had been telling their readers for some months that the President's proposals, which had been reintroduced into the Eighty-Eighth Congress as an omnibus education bill, were indeed dead as a doornail. How this came to be is the subject of this case.

D EVELOPING and defining the "program of the President" is a complicated process under the best of circumstances. For an incoming President, involved in the complexities of a transition in Administration, it is especially difficult. As President-elect, John F. Kennedy faced the problems of recruiting and staffing the top positions of the Executive Branch, and preparing to face pressing problems in the areas of foreign policy (for example, on Cuba and Laos) and domestic economic policy. Had time permitted—and in government it too seldom does—a thorough analysis of the trends in American education in the winter of 1960–61 might well have suggested that the education "issue" was also in a state of transition.

The President's Program

President Kennedy was bringing to the White House a considerable first-hand body of experience with the politics of aid to education. In both the House and the Senate he had served on the committees dealing with education legislation. In the course of the 1960 campaign he had repeatedly endorsed federal aid for both school construction and teacher salaries. (Nixon had supported aid to school construction only.) He had also emphasized that he favored such aid for public schools only and opposed granting federal funds to parochial schools. In his widely quoted speech to the Greater Houston Ministerial Association he had stated: "I believe in an America where the separation of church and state is absolute—where no church or church school is granted any public funds." This statement had not allayed the fears of all Protestants—though it had disturbed some Catholic leaders—and it added to the range of policy constraints within which the President could operate.

Issues and Interest Groups: Federal Aid to Schools?

Kennedy's stand on education had been lauded during the campaign by the National Education Association. The NEA, with a total membership of around 700,000 teachers and school superintendents, is particularly concerned with aid to teacher salaries. It has been campaigning for federal aid for public schools for several decades. Over the years it has emphasized that teaching should be regarded as a profession and pay accordingly. It has opposed the idea of union-style collective bargaining by teachers. The NEA is organized on a state-by-state "federal" basis, with some state branches giving more attention to political activity at the state level than at the national. Although it maintains large, modernistic headquarters in Washington, it is widely regarded as a rather ineffective lobby. Its chief competitor as a spokesman for teachers is the American Federation of Teachers, which is affiliated with the AFL-CIO. This latter organization is the dominant teacher organization in many big cities and uses collective-bargaining techniques. In addition there is a separate National Catholic Education Association, as well as a major separate teacher organization in California.

Other major groups generally supporting federal aid to education have been the AFL-CIO, the Americans for Democratic Action, the National Congress of Parent-Teachers Associations, the American Association of University Women, the Council of Chief State School Officers, the American Association of University Professors, the American Parents' Committee, the United Mine Workers, and the National Farmers' Union. The National Association for the Advancement of Colored People has supported federal aid provided that it goes only to nonsegregated schools.
[*groups supporting*]

During the 1950's the National Catholic Welfare Conference affirmed its "traditional opposition to outright continuing Federal support for education" and to "the use of Federal funds for teachers' salaries." To some extent federal aid for public-school teacher salaries would inevitably increase the financial pinch being felt by the parochial schools. With a limited supply of teaching nuns, the Catholic schools are having to hire an increasing number of lay teachers at more or less competitive rates.

In recent years outright opposition to school aid has been a special concern of the United States Chamber of Commerce. The Chamber has vigorously opposed school-aid bills in testimony before Congress and has helped to organize effective state and local opposition. Like the NEA, the Chamber devotes considerable time, money, and personnel to preparing research material on education. Other major groups generally opposing federal aid have included the National Association of Manufacturers, the Council of State Chambers of Commerce, the Farm Bureau, the American Legion, the Daughters of the American Revolution, the Investment Bankers Association of America, and the Southern States Industrial Council.
[*groups opposing*]

The President's Task Force on Education

Shortly after the 1960 election, Kennedy named a number of special advisory task forces to study various substantive policy areas. Among these was a task force on education. The chairman of the six-man group was Frederick Hovde, president of Purdue University and a leading figure in the State Universities Association. The other five members represented other points of view within the educational world, but included no spokesmen for the conservative, Southern Democratic, Catholic church, or NAACP positions. The report of the task force on education recommended three major legislative proposals:

1. Federal support for the public-school system. Here the task force recommended general aid of $30 per year for each pupil in average daily attendance in public schools (cost: $1.2 billion per year). In addition, it recommended an added $20 per child for states with personal income per student below 70 per cent of the national average (cost: $140 million), and also an added $20 per child in the public schools of those cities with over 300,000 population (cost: $120 million per year).

2. Federal support for housing and academic facilities for colleges and universities. Here the group called for expansion of the existing college-housing loan program, and establishment of a new program of both grants and loans for construction of academic facilities, such as classrooms and libraries.

3. Federal support to strengthen the National Defense Education Act. Here the group recommended general extension of the NDEA program, with increased loan funds for college students, elimination of the controversial non-Communist affidavit, and extension of the forgiveness feature on loans to all teachers (rather than merely those going on to teach in public schools).

The reaction of many Catholic church leaders to these proposals was strongly negative. As the day for Kennedy's inauguration approached, Catholic press criticism of the Hovde recommendations mounted. On January 17, three days before the inauguration, these recommendations were the subject of a major address by Francis Cardinal Spellman of New York:

> I believe and I state that these recommendations are unfair to most parents of the nation's 6,800,000 parochial and private school children. Such legislation would discriminate against a multitude of America's children because their parents choose to exercise their constitutional right to educate them in accordance with their religious beliefs. . . .
> I cannot believe that Congress would accept the proposals of the task force and use economic compulsion to force parents to relinquish their rights to have religion taught to their children.

I cannot believe that Congress would enact a program of financial assistance and secondary education unless all children were granted equal educational privileges, regardless of the school they attend.

By denying this measure of equality to church-related school children and their parents, the task force proposals are blatantly discriminating against them, depriving them of freedom of mind and freedom of religion.

If Congress were to comply with the task force proposals as outlined by this committee (and once again I express my faith that Congress would not do so), and compel a child to attend a State school as a condition for sharing in education funds, it would be engaging in thought control.

The seventy-one-year-old Cardinal, who had tangled on this subject with Mrs. Eleanor Roosevelt and Congressman Graham Barden a decade earlier, was yielding no ground to his forty-three-year-old coreligionist, the President-elect.

A "New Frontier" for Education?

Whether the task-force report had been intended as a trial balloon or not, it served to indicate stormy weather for the President's aid-to-education proposals. Both the President and his Secretary of Health, Education and Welfare (HEW), Abraham Ribicoff, had been in the House of Representatives during the bitter parochial-school dispute of 1949–50. So had several of the key Congressmen involved in working out the details of the program. But there seemed no simple alternative that would avoid even more certain dangers.

On February 20 the President sent his Message on Education to Congress, and the draft of the proposed school-aid bill was ready soon thereafter. Neither the Message nor the draft of the bill indicated any concessions to supporters of aid for nonpublic schools. Priorities of both funds and timing would be given to the needs of public schools over those of higher education. The gist of the Message in regard to school aid was as follows:

I recommend to the Congress a 3-year program of general Federal assistance for public elementary and secondary classroom construction and teachers' salaries.

Based essentially on the bill which passed the Senate last year (S. 8), although beginning at a more modest level of expenditures, this program would assure every State of no less than $15 for every public school student in average daily attendance, with the total amount appropriated ($666 million being authorized in the first year, rising to $866 million over a 3-year period) distributed according to the equalization formula contained in the last year's Senate bill. . . .

The bill which will follow this message has been carefully drawn to eliminate disproportionately large or small inequities, and to make the maximum use of a limited number of dollars. In accordance with the clear prohibition of the Constitution, no elementary or secondary school funds are allocated for constructing church schools or paying church school teachers' salaries; and thus non-public school children are rightfully not counted in determining the funds each State will receive for its public schools. . . .

. . . For some 40 years, the Congress has wrestled with this problem and searched for a workable solution. I believe that we now have such a solution; and that this Congress in this year will make a landmark contribution to American education.

In regard to higher education, the President's message went on to request extension of the college-housing loan program, establishment of a similar loan program for the construction of academic facilities at both public and private institutions, and establishment of a program of state-administered undergraduate scholarships. (Federal funds would be allocated to the states, which would award stipends of up to $1,000 to students chosen on the basis of ability and need, who would be free to attend the college of their choice.)

but these "scholarships" ... must be repaid

On its proposals for teacher salary aid and undergraduate scholarships the Administration could expect little Republican support—a substantial number of Republicans might be won over to a one-time school-construction bill or to an academic-facilities bill, but not to salary aid or scholarships. The Administration did have one tactical innovation, however, that control of the Presidency made available. This was the idea of tying in the school-aid bill with renewal of the popular program of federal aid for "impacted areas." The latter program had been set up to assist local school districts where a major military, naval, or other federal installation took much of the land off the tax rolls and at the same time generated a tremendous increase in school enrollments. In 1950, after the failure of a drive for general school aid, Congress had given regular authorization to the programs of federal assistance both for school construction (under Public Law 81-815) and for operating expenses (under Public Law 81-874) in areas where there was such a federal "impact."

Like many other federal programs, the impacted-areas statutes were authorized for only a limited number of years. This procedure gives both supporters and opponents a chance to modify a measure, and gives Congress as a whole a useful weapon in dealing with the Executive Branch. When the programs had come up for renewal in 1958 the more essential part, providing aid for children of parents both working and residing on federal property, had been made permanent. But the remaining provisions, which provided something of a windfall for many school districts, would expire again on June 30, 1961.

The Administration would, in effect, be holding the expiring portions of the impacted-areas programs as a hostage to help force through the general school-aid bill. If this "package" approach had a tactical appeal to Democratic strategists in the House, it also made a certain amount of bureaucratic sense to HEW officials. If the President's bill were adopted, it would funnel federal funds to the states, but certain school districts within the states would also be receiving additional federal funds directly under the impacted-areas program. It seemed rational to cut the impacted-areas aid back enough to take account of the new general federal aid. Hence at a meeting in Palm Beach, Florida, in December 1960 Kennedy had accepted the idea of the "package" approach.

When finally ready for introduction the Administration bill ran to twenty-nine double-spaced pages. It was introduced in the House by Congressman Frank Thompson (Democrat of New Jersey) and became H.R. 4970. Ordinarily an Administration bill is introduced by the appropriate subcommittee chairman, but in the House this was Congressman Cleveland M. Bailey, a West Virginia Protestant. Ever since the bitter religious controversy of 1949–50 it had been standard practice to have public-school bills introduced by a Catholic Congressman, thus foreclosing at least one form of criticism. Thompson was both a supporter of the Administration bill—having played a key role in its drafting—and a Roman Catholic.

In the Senate the Administration bill was introduced by the appropriate subcommittee chairman, Senator Wayne Morse (Democrat of Oregon). In the Senate—but not in the House—additional members can cosponsor a measure. Within a week twenty-one additional Democrats (including only two from the South—Fulbright of Arkansas and Yarborough of Texas) had signed on as cosponsors. Morse was an ardent supporter of federal aid for both construction and teacher salaries but was also known for his support of some form of aid for nonpublic schools. Moreover, he had the reputation of being one of the most individualistic, even erratic, men in a highly individualistic body. No one questioned Morse's intellectual ability (except Clare Booth Luce, who in an angry moment had suggested that his problems stemmed from having been kicked in the head by a horse), but in his sixteen years in the Senate, he had never had the responsibility for managing a major Administration bill.

The Catholic Hierarchy Dissents

When the President's Message on Education went to Congress on February 20, 1961, the lines of conflict were quick to form. Ordinarily one of the functions of committee hearings is to elicit the views of various affected interests and groups. But no one felt compelled to wait for the hearings on education—the issues were familiar ones and most views were already crystallized. On the non-Catholic side a spokesman for the Protestants and

Other Americans United for Separation of Church and State (POAU) greeted the message with enthusiasm: "We congratulate the President for declaring that direct Federal aid to church schools at the elementary and secondary levels is unconstitutional." On the Catholic side, the Most Reverend Lawrence J. Shehan, Bishop of Bridgeport, Connecticut (and chairman of the Department of Education of the National Catholic Welfare Conference), expressed "keen disappointment" that the President had excluded private and parochial schools. Conceding that there were "certain constitutional problems," the Bishop asked: "Is there not ingenuity enough in the Federal Government to devise an acceptable course that would safeguard the Constitution and meet, at least to some extent, the needs of all children?"

Catholic criticism of the Kennedy proposals mounted rapidly, especially in various Catholic diocesan newspapers. Congressmen, especially those from urban areas in the Northeast, began to receive substantial amounts of mail from parents of parochial-school students. An authoritative statement of the position of the Catholic hierarchy was soon forthcoming from the administrative board of the National Catholic Welfare Conference. The board, consisting of the five cardinals of the American Catholic Church plus the ten archbishops and bishops who head departments (of which education is one) of the conference, met in Washington on March 1 in a closed session. Following the meeting Archbishop Karl J. Alter, chairman of the administrative board, released the following statement:

> Yesterday the Administrative Board met and considered in addition to the routine questions the particular problem of Federal aid to education. In the absence of the official minutes I think I can summarize the discussion fairly and briefly as follows:
>
> 1. The question of whether or not there ought to be Federal aid is a judgment to be based on objective economic facts connected with the schools of the country and consequently Catholics are free to take a position in accordance with the facts.
>
> 2. In the event that there is Federal aid to education we are deeply convinced that in justice Catholic school children should be given the right to participate.
>
> 3. Respecting the form of participation, we hold it to be strictly within the framework of the Constitution that long-term, low-interest loans to private institutions could be part of the Federal aid program. It is proposed, therefore, that an effort be made to have an amendment to this effect attached to the bill.
>
> 4. In the event that a federal aid program is enacted which excludes children in private schools these children will be victims of discriminatory legislation. There will be no alternative but to oppose such discrimination.

Press reaction to the hierarchy's statement was mixed. Many Protestant and Jewish spokesmen expressed shock that the hierarchy seemed willing, in effect, to kill the President's public-school bill unless some aid to parochial schools was included. In a widely quoted column, New York *Times* correspondent James Reston saw the move as one likely "to hurt both religion and education." But Reston went on to add:

> The claims of the Catholic Church cannot be lightly brushed aside, as President Kennedy originally tried to push them aside, by saying that aid to parochial schools was "clearly unconstitutional" and by adding that "there isn't any room for debate on that subject." This merely envenoms the debate that is now obviously in progress.
>
> The main reason for Federal aid in the first place was to see to it that the Nation develops all the brains it has, and if this reason is valid, it surely needs Catholic brains as well as Baptist or Presbyterian brains.

At his March 8 White House press conference the subject of possible loans for parochial schools took up almost a third of the time. The President repeated that he felt there was no room for debate in regard to grants, and that "by my reading of the constitutional judgments [in the *Everson* v. *New Jersey* Supreme Court decision on public aid for parochial students' bus transportation], my judgment has been that across-the-board loans are also unconstitutional." He added, however, "There have been some kinds of loans to nonpublic schools which have been supported by the Congress and signed by the President and about which no constitutional problem has yet been raised, and the National Defense Education Act is the best example."

The sharpness of the split between the President and the Catholic hierarchy was somewhat surprising. The existence of some divergence of views, however, was less surprising. The young President was a millionaire's son, a Harvard College graduate (who had never attended parochial schools), and a man who obviously enjoyed the companionship of assorted Harvard intellectuals. He was not a product of expressly Catholic institutions and culture who had gone into politics. Rather, he was a politician who happened—probably to his advantage—to be a Catholic. His greatest love was politics (in which he pursued success with all the passion of a man possessed by what Max Weber termed the "Protestant ethic").

By contrast the leaders of the American Catholic church have generally been, in the secular sense, self-made men. They have come from homes of moderate or less-than-moderate means. As Archbishop (now Cardinal) Richard Cushing pointed out in 1947,

> in all the American hierarchy, resident in the United States, there is not known to me one Bishop, Archbishop or Cardinal whose father or mother

was a college graduate. Every one of our Bishops and Archbishops is the son of a working man and a working man's wife.

Leadership in the Catholic church, somewhat like leadership in Congress, generally comes only with age. Many of the top members of the hierarchy had been roughly contemporary with Al Smith. It would be surprising if an influential part of the hierarchy had not regarded Kennedy as the wrong Catholic running for the wrong office at the wrong time.

A man much more in tune with the thinking of the hierarchy was Congressman John McCormack, the House majority floor leader. He had entered Congress in 1928—the year of Al Smith's defeat—and was a devout Catholic and recipient of several Catholic honorary awards. He had been serving as Democratic majority leader before Kennedy had been first elected to the House. There had been friction between the two first while Kennedy was in the House, and then later over politics in Massachusetts. Hence there was a minimum of surprise when, in a March 5 radio interview, McCormack called for "long-term loans at reasonable rates of interest for the construction or the renovation or the repair of private schools." In the House the influence of the sixty-nine-year-old McCormack was not to be taken lightly. The President might well reflect that in regard to aid for education his problems were coming not singly but in battalions.

Congress and Aid to Schools: The 1961 Story

The first major hurdle for the President's school-aid bill would come in the hearings of the committees to which the legislation had been routinely referred—the House Committee on Education and Labor and the Senate Committee on Labor and Public Welfare. These standing committees, which were created under the Legislative Reorganization Act of 1946, have roughly similar jurisdictions covering both labor legislation and most education measures. The Senate committee has a slightly broader scope since it handles certain bills relating to public health (such as aid for medical and dental schools and students) which in the House go to the Committee on Interstate and Foreign Commerce. (In both chambers the college-dormitory loan program has been handled as part of general housing legislation by the respective Committees on Banking and Currency, which in 1959 had unsuccessfully sought also to provide loans for college academic facilities.)

In both House and Senate the committees dealing with labor and education are of only modest prestige, and membership on them is not regarded as a prize assignment. Indeed, in the House the Education and Labor Committee has been notorious for its extreme partisanship, contentious members, bitter conflicts, procedural wrangling, and general lack of influence with the House membership. This style of operation developed early—in its first year of operation the committee fought over the Taft-Hartley Act—and has influenced subsequent recruitment of new members. The Republican leadership has sought to "pack" the committee with staunch pro-management men; the Democratic leadership has sought to "pack" it with equally staunch pro-union men. Political "moderates" have seldom gone on the committee or have transferred off as soon as possible.

After the 1958 Democratic sweep, the party ratio on the Education and Labor Committee had been shifted to increase the number of Democrats. With only a handful of Southern Democrats on the committee the liberal Democrats had fought with their conservative chairman, Graham Barden (Democrat of North Carolina). In 1960 Barden had retired, and under the inexorable rule of seniority the chairmanship had passed to Adam Clayton Powell (Democrat of New York), the controversial Harlem minister-politician. But the liberal Democrats had lost several of their most skillful legislative tacticians: Lee Metcalf had transferred to a more important committee and had then been elected to the Senate; Stewart Udall had been named Secretary of the Interior; and Carl Elliott, an Alabama liberal with a special interest in education, had been tapped by Speaker Rayburn for service on the vital House Rules Committee. Their absence from the committee was likely to be sorely felt by the remaining school-aid supporters.

Senate Committee Hearings: Harmony Prevails

Senate hearings on the school-aid bill opened on the morning of March 8 (the same day that the Presidential press conference concentrated on the parochial-school question). Senator Wayne Morse presided, and most of the education subcommittee members were present. The hearings were open to the public. The senators were seated somewhat like judges behind a semicircular dais. There was a table for the witness who was testifying, and there were additional tables for the press. The membership of the subcommittee, in order of seniority, was as follows:

DEMOCRATS	REPUBLICANS
WAYNE MORSE (Ore.), *Chairman*	CLIFFORD P. CASE (N.J.)
LISTER HILL (Ala.)	JACOB K. JAVITS (N.Y.)
PAT McNAMARA (Mich.)	BARRY GOLDWATER (Ariz.)
RALPH W. YARBOROUGH (Tex.)	
JOSEPH S. CLARK (Pa.)	
JENNINGS RANDOLPH (W. Va.)	

Of the subcommittee members only Goldwater was generally opposed to a substantial federal-aid program. There seemed little doubt that the group would vote for something close to the Administration's recommendations by a heavy majority.

Both the Senate hearings and the later floor debate were to reflect the particular style of Senator Morse. As a former law-school dean, Morse seemed to perceive his role of chairman as quasi-judicial. He intended to prepare a sound "record" on which Senatorial judgments could be based and regarded himself as "counsel" to the President in regard to the school-aid bill. He was also very conscious of his role as a spokesman for the Administration; he even spoke of himself as being "a private" in the ranks of the President's supporters. This uncharacteristic attitude was not to last, but for the time being Morse was evidently enjoying the responsibility—and the power—that goes with handling a major piece of legislation.

The Administration's leadoff witness was Secretary Ribicoff, accompanied by the usual phalanx of departmental assistants. After he had made a general presentation of the Administration's position Morse entered a request for information:

> I think you well know that there will probably be introduced an amendment to this bill which would seek to provide interest-bearing loans to private schools . . . I would like to ask the administration, through your office, to prepare a brief for this committee setting forth the position of the administration on the constitutional questions and other legal questions raised by such an amendment.

This request was then broadened to include a memorandum indicating "the Federal aid which now goes to private institutions, denominational and otherwise, in this country, to hospitals, institutions of higher learning, private foundations, and the like. . . ." Work on this material was to keep lawyers of both HEW and the Justice Department busy for most of the next three weeks.

Before the committee adjourned for the morning there was one touch of comic relief. Morse, in a statement that was to become the basis for a humorous column by a Washington *Post* writer, said that he had a request "from one group that wanted to appear as witnesses before this committee in historic costume, and I have notified them that this committee room is not a theater or a stage." The particular individuals were not identified, but apparently they were opposed to any aid for parochial schools. They had planned to appear in costume as Madison and Jefferson, as the *Post* columnist put it, in order to portray how the founding fathers would roll over in their graves at the thought of aiding parochial schools. Whatever their intention, it did not accord with Morse's concept of orderly committee procedure.

The second day of Senate hearings was given over to officials of the National Education Association, the executive secretary of the Council of Chief State School Officers (a key group in administering any grant-in-aid program), and Senator E. L. Bartlett (Democrat of Alaska), who was concerned over the effect of the allocation formula on Alaska, where building costs are exceptionally high. The witnesses appearing for the NEA were old hands at the subject and received friendly questioning.

Dr. Edgar Fuller, appearing for the Council of Chief State School Officers, indicated that he had replies from a survey of state school superintendents (or their equivalent) and that most favored the bill. There were, however, significant suggestions and exceptions. He also pointed out that the lack of a federal school-aid program was complicating the problem of financing education at the state level because of the proliferation of other federal grant programs. As Dr. Fuller put it:

> If they want to spend a dollar for highways, they can get 9 Federal dollars. If they are willing to pull out the billboards, it will be 9 dollars plus. If they want to extend their welfare or health services, they can get matching money from the Federal Government to help them to do it. If they want to build hospitals, they can in many instances get 3 dollars of Federal money for each dollar of their own. And so on through the list.
>
> This gives the services which are competing for the State dollar in State legislatures a very great advantage over education. If they vote 1 dollar for education, education gets 1 dollar. If they vote 1 dollar for roads, roads gets 10 dollars. . . . This competition has made it hard to get money at the State level for education.

On the third day of hearings the level of controversy began to pick up, although opponents of aid for parochial schools found themselves without a clear target to focus on. By scheduling the spokesmen in favor of parochial-school aid for the final day of hearings, Morse was skillfully minimizing the likelihood of open conflict in the hearings. Opponents of parochial-school aid testifying at this hearing included the Grand Master of the Masonic Lodge for Puerto Rico and spokesmen for the Baptist Joint Committee on Public Affairs and the American Jewish Congress. The strongest statement, however, came from C. Stanley Lowell, associate director of the Protestants and Other Americans United for Separation of Church and State (POAU). He presented a variation on the familiar theme of the dangers of letting the camel get his nose under the tent:

> I should like to call attention to the end result of a program of grants to church schools or loans to church schools. Once the Congress reverses our tradition and embarks upon such a course, it will find that turning back is extremely difficult. The movement tends to be the other way. From small loans to large grants—so the process unfolds—until the taxpayers are charged with the entire bill for these schools.

Mr. Lowell went on to cite an editorial from the February 1 issue of *Christian Century,* a leading Protestant publication. The editorial stated:

Cardinal Spellman has not changed his mind. His aim is still to compel Protestants, Jews, and others to support a wholly controlled function of the Roman Catholic Church. The compulsion lies in the use of the taxing powers of the Federal Government to raise funds for Catholic schools. He has given us fair warning, so he should have our answer. American Protestants will never pay taxes to support Catholic schools. We will oppose enactment of laws which require such payments. If Congress is pressured into enacting such laws, we will contest them in the courts. If the courts reverse themselves and declare such laws constitutional, we will still refuse to pay these taxes, paying whatever price is necessary to preserve religious liberty in a pluralistic society.

Lowell agreed with Senator Morse that this was "strong language," but he went on to add:

I can assure you it would be among the mildest expressions on record should the Congress initiate a program of taxing all citizens to pay for religious teaching. This program would provoke such outbreaks of intercreedal vituperation as would hitherto have been deemed impossible among us.

Amid all the hue and cry over the religious question, a spokesman for the NAACP found little response to his concern over granting federal funds to Southern states that were opposing integration. Congressman Powell had already agreed not to introduce his controversial "Powell amendment" (designed to prohibit aid to segregated schools), and Senator Morse was quick to make his opposition known:

I indicated the other day I am not a mathematician, but I can count Congressional noses. I do not think, contrary to your opinion, that there is any chance of passing the administration bill with the civil rights amendment added to it. I think that failure would be most unfortunate, because our real need, in my judgment, is to get the principle of Federal aid to elementary and secondary education on the statute books of this country. We can then proceed, in independent legislation, to see to it that our educational program is carried out in accordance with the constitutional rights of all citizens.

Morse, in a philosophic moment, wondered "to what extent a Senator presiding over a meeting really has any right to give advice." After indicating that this was "an individual judgment," he continued:

I shall speak to the hierarchy of the Catholic Church who will be testifying before us later. I think the leadership of that denomination has a great opportunity to say, in effect, to the American people: "We are willing to agree that we should start with the public school system and, therefore, we are going to urge the passage of this public school law without any amendments added to it which are likely to endanger the passage of any legislation at all. We also reserve our right to carry out what we think is our duty to press the Congress of the United States for the passage of a separate and independent bill which raises the question as to whether or not loans which yield sufficient interest to pay for the cost of the use of money are constitutional."

Morse added, "It is a little presumptuous for a Senator to be giving gratuitous advice," but he would take the risk.

At almost the same time that Morse was offering his "advice," Cardinal Spellman was issuing an additional statement of his views in New York. The Cardinal was "still opposed to any program of Federal aid that would penalize a multitude of America's children" because they attended parochial schools. The Cardinal concluded that "equivalent benefits to children attending private and church-related schools" without violating the Constitution "would seem to be an attainable objective." The specifics were "matters for the discretion of Congress."

The dramatic high point of the Senate hearings came when Monsignor Hochwalt presented the case for the Catholic bishops. His testimony was along lines similar to that of Cardinal Spellman. The Monsignor began by pointing out the scope of the Catholic school system: some 10,300 elementary schools, plus about 2,400 high schools, with a combined staff of 102,000 and enrollments totaling over 5 million students. He continued:

> These schools are established, operated, and maintained by Catholic citizens, by people of the same income group as those living about the neighboring public schools.
>
> They are integrally a part of what is basically a dual system. Public and private schools form a necessary partnership for the fruitful service of this country. We are one people and it is in our national interest that both systems make their full contribution in the service of our children. Any other attitude would be extremely shortsighted and self-defeating.
>
> A great many parents of parochial school children would welcome Federal aid as a necessary help to them in a time of financial strain. They do feel the double burden of supporting two school systems, and are apt to inquire much more pointedly now than heretofore why the proponents of Federal aid do not take into consideration their needs. They point out that the classroom shortage exists as demonstrably in the private school system as it does in the public school system.
>
> What can be done for the private school and in particular the parochial school?

Senator Morse commended the Monsignor on the "objectivity" and "fairness" of his statement, adding "that this committee must face up to this problem." But Monsignor Hochwalt had reservations about having public-school and parochial-school problems dealt with in separate legislation:

I have a feeling that one measure would pass in this Congress, the Federal aid as such. I have a feeling that a second measure, which would provide for our schools, wouldn't have much of a chance.

Therefore, it seems to us that our welfare should be considered in tandem with the administration bill in some fashion so that that can be done.

Morse agreed that "if I were sitting in your position, I would be rather inclined to hold tenaciously to the point of view you just expressed." But, he continued, we "have some differences in responsibilities." With this the Monsignor agreed, and shortly thereafter the session adjourned for lunch (without extensive questioning of the Monsignor by the Southern Democrats on the subcommittee).

Senate hearings had to be reopened on March 20 to accommodate additional Protestant spokesmen, who were opposed to any aid for parochial schools. Among those testifying were Robert E. Van Dusen, of the National Lutheran Council, and James DeForest Murch, of the National Association of Evangelicals. Gerald E. Knoff's view was typical: "The present controversy is not of our choosing. The National Council of Churches did not raise the issue. Yet a principle is at stake. If Roman Catholic leaders raise their demand as a moral issue, Protestant leaders must reply that they oppose the proposal as a moral issue." Morse reiterated his own view that although outright grants to nonpublic schools would be unconstitutional, "There is no constitutional violation as long as there is, in fact, no subsidy." Although a loan program would be legally acceptable, so far as Morse was concerned, the "politics of the situation" was something else:

> I well know, and I think many in this room will agree with me, that if we have both public grant and private loan mixed in this bill, the odds are against any bill at all. I repeat again this morning; I will repeat up to the last minute of these hearings; I will repeat in executive session; and I will repeat on the floor of the Senate, that I am not going to support private schools in an attempt to add a loan amendment to this bill. I think it would defeat a public school bill.

Obviously the Administration faced a problem not only in the form of possible aid for nonpublic schools, but also in the procedure to be followed in considering such a program. The President's attempt to avoid the issue by invoking constitutional doctrine had failed. It would take time to work out a second line of defense.

House Committee Hearings: The Perils of Partisanship

On the other side of the Capitol, things were not proceeding so smoothly. Morse had skillfully conducted the Senate hearings in a manner designed to minimize conflict, develop possible grounds of compromise, and offend none of his fellow committee members. But this is not the manner in which the House Committee on Education and Labor usually operates. Its members are more likely to maximize conflict, avoid areas of possible compromise, and engage in personal recriminations at the drop of a hat.

Committee chairman Adam Clayton Powell had moved to shake up the committee in a variety of ways. He had expanded the size of the Democrat-controlled committee staff; he had brought in his top secretary as committee clerk (promoting the newlywed Mrs. Powell, who remained in his office, from $3,074 to $12,974 a year); and he had sought to take over part of the minority party staff's office space (in which the ranking Republican member, Carroll Kearns of Pennsylvania, had barricaded himself for a time). Powell had also moved to reorganize the subcommittee system. Powell had established not just one subcommittee to handle education legislation—as on the Senate side—but three: a Subcommittee on General Education (with Cleveland Bailey as chairman and Frank Thompson as second-ranking Democrat); a Subcommittee on Special Education (with Edith Green, Democrat of Oregon, as chairwoman); and a Select Subcommittee on Education (with Frank Thompson as chairman).

he's in trouble for that now, boy!

This multiplication of subcommittees created some institutional rivalry and complicated the process of setting priorities among the various education proposals. Thus Congresswoman Green, a strong supporter of aid for higher education, moved to commence hearings on the Administration bill in that field (H.R. 5266, which she had introduced) the same week that Bailey and Thompson were to open hearings on the general school-aid bill. Congresswoman Green wanted to get the relatively noncontroversial higher-education bill out of the way before tackling the more explosive school-aid measure; Thompson wanted to give the school-aid bill priority. Although Congresswoman Green went ahead with the hearings on higher education (held on March 15, 16, and 17), Thompson's view—which reflected the Administration's priorities—was to prevail.

School-aid hearings in the House began, rather inauspiciously, on March 13. The membership of the General Education Subcommittee consisted of the following:

DEMOCRATS	REPUBLICANS
CLEVELAND M. BAILEY (W. Va.), *Chairman*	PETER FRELINGHUYSEN (N.J.)
FRANK THOMPSON, JR. (N.J.)	ALBERT H. QUIE (Minn.)
JOHN BRADEMAS (Ind.)	PETER A. GARLAND (Me.)
JAMES G. O'HARA (Mich.)	
RALPH J. SCOTT (N. C.)	

Bailey began the session by welcoming the three newly appointed members of the subcommittee and then laid down some rules of procedure: witnesses should submit fifty copies of their statements, be prepared to summarize their statements orally, and expect questions from the committee members, who would be subject to the House's customary "five-minute rule" limiting each member to that amount of time. Bailey also indicated that to "prevent repetition of testimony," public witnesses would be limited to spokesmen for national organizations.

Secretary Ribicoff was to be the first witness, but before he could get started, Congressman Frelinghuysen objected that the subcommittee had not held any previous meetings and hence could hardly have laid down ground rules for witnesses. He also complained that he and other minority members had received no list of witnesses scheduled to appear, and since many members were on many of the new subcommittees he would like to know what the schedule of meetings was to be. Bailey brushed Frelinghuysen's complaints aside and turned the proceedings over to second-ranking Frank Thompson.

Frelinghuysen and Thompson represented adjoining districts in New Jersey, but they had sharply different—often clashing—personalities. Frelinghuysen was a progressive Republican who had consistently supported aid for school construction but was highly critical of the Administration bill. A *magna cum laude* graduate of Princeton, Frelinghuysen sometimes seemed to approach issues more in the spirit of academic research than of down-to-earth politics. He was, for example, plainly shocked at the Administration's coupling of school aid with extension of the impacted-areas program, and he was dubious that the President's "modest program" could have a significant effect on both school construction and teacher salaries. Frank Thompson, by contrast, was a tough-minded liberal Democrat. A former minority leader of the lower house of the New Jersey legislature, Thompson had moved ahead rapidly in the House. Although a highly intelligent and cultured man (he was one of the leaders in the campaign for a Federal Advisory Council on the Arts), Thompson was a blunt-spoken man who approached politics with something of the same vigor and combativeness for which he had been decorated at Iwo Jima.

Much of the questioning in the House hearings repeated ground already covered in the Senate hearings. There was, however, an obvious sense of partisanship and frustration not prevalent in the Senate hearings. By holding sessions every day, the subcommittee heard most of the major public witnesses by the end of the week. These included Paul Blanshard for POAU (against the bill), spokesmen for the NEA (in favor of the bill) and for the United States Chamber of Commerce (against the bill), the president of the New York City Board of Education (who asked for aid for nonpublic schools, thus arousing a storm of criticism in New York), Michigan's Governor Swainson (in favor of the bill), Gerald Knoff for the National Council of Churches and Robert Van Deusen for the National Lutheran

Council (who both opposed aid for parochial schools), and Monsignor Hochwalt (who presented the case for the parochial schools).

A second week of hearings was devoted largely to members of Congress, most of whom made short appearances in support of full-scale payment of the impacted-areas funds. Support for this program was so strong that Congressman Thompson concluded that "if this bill fails with 815 and 874 in it, this subcommittee would need nothing more, having had all this testimony, than to reconvene after that tragedy, report out 815 and 874 and it will go through on the consent calendar."

Major appearances before the House subcommittee were also made by Senator Barry Goldwater, who was sharply questioned by both Thompson and Congressman John Brademas (Democrat of Indiana), and by Arthur S. Flemming, who had been Eisenhower's last HEW Secretary. Although Eisenhower was subsequently to denounce the bill, Flemming generally supported it. Final committee hearings were held on March 29, just before the Easter recess. Rabbi Morris Sherer, representing Agudath Israel (a national organization of orthodox Jews), testified in favor of aid for nonpublic schools. His testimony contrasted with the opposition voiced by reform and conservative Jewish denominations and the Jewish civic organizations. In all, the House subcommittee heard seventy-nine witnesses in person and received statements, letters, and resolutions from many others. The public hearings had raised a great many problems for supporters of school aid; they had not indicated any easy solutions.

The Parochial-School Issue: Search for Compromise

By the end of March the tactical situation could be summarized as follows. The campaign for public-school aid was in serious trouble. Supporters of the Catholic hierarchy were, in effect, in a position to veto the Administration's public-school bill. The President—keenly aware of his sensitive position as the first Roman Catholic to be elected to the Presidency—was unlikely to exert any public pressure to win concessions for a loan program for parochial schools. And it was entirely possible that opponents of parochial-school aid were also, in effect, in a position to veto any such proposal.

The brief that Senator Morse had requested from Secretary Ribicoff on the church-state issue was released on March 28. In general it supported the President's view that outright grants or across-the-board loans for nonpublic schools were unconstitutional. It went on to argue that the existing programs of aid for parochial schools (or for students who attended parochial schools) typically either "bear a clear-cut relationship to children's health or promote a special purpose with a clear national defense implication." The former would cover grants for textbooks or for bus transportation (both of which the Supreme Court had upheld) as well as the hot-school-lunch program (which had not been litigated). The latter rationale would, the brief argued, cover programs such as the 1958 National Defense Education Act, which "permits the U.S. Commissioner of Education to make loans to private schools to acquire science, mathematics, or foreign language equipment."

Since this NDEA loan program was to be widely cited in the course of arguments over aid for parochial schools, it is worth noting that it had been adopted under rather unusual circumstances. The original NDEA bill had made no provisions for such loans, and no witnesses or testimony were heard on the subject. The provision had been added at the last minute in the Senate committee's "markup" of the bill (the review of a bill's actual language for final changes or approval in closed session). There was no floor debate over the provision, which was retained in the final conference report. The amount of such loans had been barely $1 million in fiscal 1960 and only $600,000 in fiscal 1961. But a small program can constitute a big precedent.

On the day following release of the HEW brief, Senators Morse and Joseph S. Clark (Democrat of Pennsylvania) introduced a "Private School Construction Loan Act" (S. 1482). The proposal more closely reflected Morse's view that interest-bearing loans for general construction were constitutional than it did the HEW brief's emphasis upon special nonsectarian purposes. The bill would have authorized forty-year loans for nonpublic schools for construction of classroom facilities. Morse indicated that he intended to hold "fair and full hearings" on the proposal, but these were ultimately canceled. The separate-bill approach did not appeal to supporters of the Catholic church position, and many Protestant groups were up in arms over the bill.

Another possibility was to amend the NDEA, which was due to expire June 30, 1962, to provide for a sort of "released time" program in reverse. If the government could lend funds for equipment to be used "to study mathematics, science, and languages," then why could it not lend funds to build classrooms for these secular purposes? This line of reasoning ignored the God-centered orientation of all instruction in parochial schools, but it seemed to offer the simplest way of keeping the hopes of parochial-school champions alive without risking the fate of the public-school bill.

On April 25 President Kennedy sent a message to Congress formally requesting extension and expansion of the NDEA. The President made no specific mention of adding loans for "special-purpose" classrooms of parochial schools, but the message left the door open for Congress to make such a change:

> Our national strength and welfare demand a strong and balanced educational system. Many proposals have been made by both public and private organizations to achieve this strength and balance.
> I am transmitting herewith draft legislation to amend, improve, and

extend the National Defense Education Act. *Some* of the recommendations of these organizations are included in the draft legislation. It is also appropriate that the Congress consider *other* proposals contained in these and other reports. [italics added]

The New York *Times,* following the school-aid fight with particular interest, gave the story a page-one headline: "COMPROMISE ON SCHOOL AID SOUGHT UNDER DEFENSE ACT."

The Administration bill was by no means over the hump, but by early May school-aid supporters were quoted as being "moderately confident that victory is in sight after a fight of more than a decade." The chief question still dividing Administration strategists was whether the NDEA amendments (including loans for special-purpose classrooms of nonpublic schools) should or should not be considered jointly with the public-school bill. Catholic spokesmen, after all, were not just interested in seeing a Congressional debate on the loan program—they wanted to see the provisions enacted into law. But Senator Morse and Congressman Thompson, the respective managers of the Administration bill, felt that joint consideration would only have the effect of killing all aid-to-education legislation.

The Senate Labor Committee met in executive session to begin final markup of the bill on May 10. That afternoon committee Democrats huddled with key Administration leaders on the touchy problems of formulas for state allocations and for counting pupils. At the meeting, in addition to key committee Democrats, were Secretary Ribicoff, Lawrence F. O'Brien (White House Congressional liaison chief), Majority Leader Mike Mansfield, Majority Whip Hubert Humphrey, and "Bobbie" Baker (omnipresent secretary to the Senate majority—a Lyndon Johnson protégé). As the Washington *Post* noted: "The makeup suggested the meeting was concerned with computing not only aid but votes."

On the following day the markup was completed. Pleas by Republican Senator Javits for his modified equalization formula were rejected. Instead the committee majority moved to drop the Administration's $15-per-student minimum and apply the equalization formula to the entire amount appropriated, with a maximum ratio (between low-income and high-income states) of three to one. The basis for counting students would be shifted from average daily attendance in public schools to total school-age population (which would give something of a bonus to states with large parochial enrollments). The committee voted to extend the impacted-areas programs virtually in their existing form, without the cutbacks requested by the Administration. The final committee vote on reporting out the revised bill was 12 to 2, with only Dirksen and Goldwater in opposition.

The House subcommittee markup of the Administration bill came on May 9. The group split 4 to 3 on straight party lines to vote down a series of amendments proposed by Republican Peter Frelinghuysen. Like the

Senate committee, the House group voted to continue the impacted-areas programs at existing levels and to compute aid on the basis of total school-age population rather than average daily attendance. Later the full House committee met in several days of closed sessions to go over the revised bill. Republican efforts to knock out aid for teacher salaries, to add an anti-segregation amendment, and to require a teacher loyalty oath (urged by California Congressman Edgar W. Hiestand, a member of the John Birch Society) were all voted down on straight party lines. The final vote to report the bill out was 18 to 13, with the minority composed of the committee's twelve Republicans plus one Southern Democrat. The majority took the option of reporting the revision out as a "clean bill" (with a new bill number: H.R. 7300). The revised bill became item 171 on the House union calendar, and would ordinarily remain there until a "special rule" providing for floor consideration was granted by the Rules Committee and adopted by the House.

The Senate Votes: The Yeas Have It

Senate debate on the school-aid bill began on May 16 and continued until May 25. Observers often suspect that floor debate is less important than decisions reached in conferences held just off the Senate floor. On the afternoon of May 16 this was quite literally true. After making the opening speech in favor of the bill, Senator Morse, who would ordinarily remain on the floor so long as the bill was under consideration, left the chamber to join Majority Leader Mansfield, Majority Whip Humphrey, and Senator Lee Metcalf in a final conference on the question of tactics: one bill or two? Also present were Secretary Ribicoff, Lawrence O'Brien, and the ubiquitous Bobbie Baker. Although Mansfield, Ribicoff, and O'Brien were reported to favor the one-bill approach, they were unable to convince Morse and the other Senators. The NDEA amendments (with the parochial-school loan provision), it was decided, would be rushed to the Senate floor soon after the public-school bill passed.

The Senate debate was unlikely to change many votes, but it could serve other purposes. To the lawyers in particular it is important in the debate, as in the hearings, to "make a record." Future administrative and perhaps judicial decisions may hinge on the evidence of what the debates indicate was "legislative intent" in regard to some ambiguous provision. A major floor speech may be made for the benefit of home consumption (Senator Herman Talmadge of Georgia was under considerable pressure from Georgia schoolteachers to support the bill despite possible segregation complications). Or a speech may be designed to garner national publicity (which may well have been in the mind of Senator Goldwater). And there is the continual round of Senatorial "mutual admiration" which makes it easier to carry on business in a body of widely differing viewpoints. And there were several proposed amendments which various Senators wanted considered. The length of time this would take was difficult to estimate in advance—Senator Mansfield, as majority leader, had been unsuccessful in his effort to enter a "unanimous-consent agreement" limiting debate on the bill to ten hours, with an additional two hours for each amendment.

The major school-aid amendments that had been proposed could be grouped into four main categories: (1) the issue of funds for segregated schools (on which four roll calls were eventually taken), (2) the modification of the state equalization formula (two roll calls), (3) the substitution of some form of tax rebate to the states in place of direct appropriations (four roll calls), and (4) the modification of the scope of the aid program—including nonpublic schools, giving aid for current operating expenses, or dropping teacher salary aid.

Of these issues the segregation question was, for the Senate, the most explosive. The legal right of the Secretary of HEW to withhold funds from a Southern state maintaining segregated schools was cloudy. Senator Strom Thurmond (Democrat of South Carolina) proposed an amendment that would flatly prohibit withholding of funds under the school-aid program because of racial segregation. This proposal was defeated, 70 to 25 (with nineteen Southern Democrats and six Republicans—including Goldwater—in the minority). A more sophisticated proposal was advanced by Georgia's Senator Talmadge. It made no mention of "segregation" but would prevent funds from being withheld from any state education agency "which has complied with the provisions of this Act." Since the Act itself included no antisegregation provision, this would amount to a Congressional prohibition against the Administration's subsequently withholding funds because of segregation—essentially a "reverse Powell amendment." This was a subtle move, but not quite subtle enough: it was voted down, 61 to 30. The minority consisted of twenty-one Southern Democrats (the remaining one was on a pair), five Republicans, and four non-Southern Democrats (including Mansfield and Metcalf).

On the antisegregation side, Senator Bush (Republican of Connecticut) introduced an amendment that was as extreme—and as unlikely to pass— as the Thurmond proposal. Bush sought to require that funds be granted only to states "proceeding toward full compliance with the constitutional requirement that racial discrimination be ended in public schools." This was voted down, 61 to 25, with twenty-one Republicans and four northern Democrats in the minority. Even Jacob Javits (Republican of New York), a leader of the civil-rights group, argued against the proposal as "unwise, untimely, prejudicial" to the chances of the bill. As Javits put it: "Notwithstanding our deep feelings about the Alabama violence, we still have to keep our eye on the ball. The ball is the passage of the education bill." A more complex antisegregation measure, seeking to authorize taxpayer's suits to prevent "unconstitutional" expenditures of funds under the school bill, was advanced by Kenneth Keating, New York's other Republican

Senator. After a spirited debate it too was defeated, 62 to 32, with thirty Republicans plus Democrats Douglas of Illinois and Hart of Michigan in the minority.

With the NDEA amendments pending as future business, the parochial-school issue attracted a minimum of concern—perhaps because the supporters of aid for parochial schools are in a much weaker position in the Senate than in the House. When Senator Goldwater forced a vote on adding loans for parochial schools, Morse's motion to table the proposed amendment was accepted, 66 to 25. Another Goldwater motion, to strike authorization for aiding teacher salaries, was defeated by a voice vote.

The only major amendment adopted by the Senate was proposed by Senator Winston L. Prouty (Republican of Vermont) and accepted by Morse. It allowed federal funds to be used to pay operating and maintenance costs, as well as construction costs or teacher salaries. The amendment was adopted, 51 to 39. Efforts to change the bill's formula for allocating funds among the various states or for basing aid on public-school enrollment figures rather than on total school-age population were less successful. Senators Javits and John Sherman Cooper (Republican of Kentucky) pressed for a roll call on their alternate equalization formula, but it was defeated, 50 to 30. Equally unsuccessful was Senator Frank Lausche (Democrat of Ohio) who was concerned about the "injustice" of counting all children when aid would actually go only for those in public schools. Whether just or unjust, the provision had major political consequences, which had been carefully weighed in both House and Senate. Use of the total school-age figure would provide more per capita assistance for public-school children in those areas with a large nonpublic school enrollment; this in turn would theoretically result in a slightly lessened local burden on *all* local parents (a point not lost on those concerned about the parochial schools). To the Senate this political advantage far outweighed any seeming irrationality or the technical problem that census figures on school-age population are only computed once every ten years (and hence become dated). Lausche's amendment was rejected, 61 to 32.

When the stockpile of proposed amendments was finally exhausted, debate on final passage of the bill itself was carried over to the next day, May 25. The outcome was a foregone conclusion by then, and the closing arguments were made before almost empty galleries, with only a handful of faithful wire-service men in the press galleries. Shortly after five o'clock, Mansfield huddled with Dirksen, then with Thurmond, to draft a final unanimous-consent agreement. It limited the remaining debate on final passage to three hours. At about seven o'clock Goldwater created a minor stir by producing a copy of the bill, already printed and bearing the notation "Passed the Senate, May 25, 1961." For once Morse was caught off guard, but aides soon brought the word that this was perfectly normal printing procedure and the bill was not fully authenticated until actually signed by the enrollment clerk (and that would wait for the official Senate vote!).

A little before eight o'clock the bells sounded for the final quorum call, then for the vote. Ordinarily many Senators are not on the floor as the roll call begins and may arrive after their names have been called. After the alphabetical roll, the chair then recognizes each Senator who is standing at his desk (the late arrivals). Some Senator, however, may still not have made it to the floor. To handle this development, especially for Senators seeking to maintain 100 per cent voting participation, the Democrats have a well-oiled process for delaying completion of the roll call for a few additional minutes. Each Senator is entitled, before the result is announced, to rise and make a parliamentary inquiry as to how he is recorded. If Bobbie Baker, the majority clerk, sees that a Democrat is missing, he passes the word to one of the Senators who has voted. That Senator pops up, is recognized, and makes a parliamentary inquiry as to how he is recorded. A chain reaction then follows (to the mystification of the gallery visitors). On final passage of the school bill, Senator Clark was detained, but after eight or ten parliamentary inquiries, he arrived.

On final passage the bill was supported by all but three of the non-Southern Democrats who voted, by almost half the Southern Democrats, and by a sprinkling of liberal Republicans. The vote was 49 to 34, with twelve additional Senators on "pairs" (six for and six against the bill). The non-Southern Democrats voting against the bill were Dodd of Connecticut (the state which fared worst under the state allocation formula), Hickey of Wyoming, and Lausche of Ohio. With the exception of Senator Russell Long of Louisiana, most Southern "moderates" supported the measure and most Southern conservatives opposed it, as indicated below:

SOUTHERNERS VOTING (OR PAIRED) *for* PASSAGE:

HILL (Ala.)
SPARKMAN (Ala.)
GORE (Tenn.)
KEFAUVER (Tenn.)
ERVIN (N.C.)
JORDAN (N.C.)
FULBRIGHT (Ark.) —
YARBOROUGH (Tex.) –
SMATHERS (Fla.) –

Ark
Tex split
Fla

SOUTHERNERS VOTING (OR PAIRED) *against* PASSAGE:

BYRD (Va.)
ROBERTSON (Va.)
THURMOND (S.C.)
JOHNSTON (S.C.)
EASTLAND (Miss.)
STENNIS (Miss.)
TALMADGE (Ga.)
RUSSELL (Ga.)
ELLENDER (La.)
LONG (La.)
McCLELLAN (Ark.) —
HOLLAND (Fla.) –
BLAKLEY (Tex.) –

A total of ten Republicans, most of them from the more liberal wing of the party, voted, paired, or announced their support of the bill on final passage:

Eastern REPUBLICANS FOR PASSAGE OF BILL:	*Other* REPUBLICANS FOR PASSAGE OF BILL:
JAVITS (N.Y.)	KUCHEL (Calif.)
CASE (N.J.)	FONG (Hawaii)
AIKEN (Vt.)	COOPER (Ky.)
PROUTY (Vt.)	WILEY (Wis.)
MRS. SMITH (Me.)	CARLSON (Kans.)

After the vote was taken there was the usual round of congratulatory speeches for Morse, and Morse gave his thanks to the hard-working professional staff of the committee. The Senate had acted; it was now up to the House. Before the final vote Majority Leader Mansfield had noted that over the past decade "a variety of obstacles, including the threat of a Presidential veto" had prevented enactment of a school-aid bill. Now, he added, "for the first time the prospects of accomplishment are bright." In regard to the situation in the House the distinguished majority leader could hardly have been more mistaken.

Trouble in the House: The "Unholy Alliance" Gets Religion

Senate passage of the Administration bill gave a psychological boost to its House supporters, but a good many other school-aid bills had cleared the Senate only to falter in the more conservatively inclined House. Ironically, the immediate problem facing school-aid strategists in the House revolved around that powerful legislative bottleneck, the Rules Committee, which had supposedly been "reformed" a bare four months earlier.

The Eighty-Seventh Congress had opened to a dramatic showdown between seventy-nine-year-old Speaker Sam Rayburn and seventy-eight-year-old Howard W. Smith (Democrat of Virginia), chairman of the Rules Committee. During the preceding two years courtly old "Judge" Smith and William Colmer (of Mississippi, the second-ranking Democrat on the committee) had frequently joined the four Republican members—all staunch conservatives—to prevent, delay, or make difficult floor consideration of liberal legislation. (For example, a school-aid bill was passed in different forms by both House and Senate, but it could not get a "rule" permitting it to go to the conference committee.) The remaining six Democrats on the twelve-man committee, each of whom had gone on the committee with Rayburn's approval, were powerless to break the six-to-six tie votes and hence unable to bring controversial bills to the floor via the regular procedure.

There had been several courses of action open to the Speaker, including procedural changes such as reinstating the twenty-one-day rule* or political changes such as altering the balance of the committee membership. With no Democratic vacancies on the committee, the latter process would require either "purging" a member or expanding the size of the committee. If someone was to be dropped, Colmer had campaigned against the Kennedy slate of electors in Mississippi, and this might be seized on as grounds for depriving him of his seat. Many liberal Democrats favored an effort to remove Colmer since this would be a "permanent" change and would also strengthen party sanctions against possible future bolts in the Deep South. But ultimately the Speaker backed away from such a direct challenge to seniority and indicated instead that he would press for adoption of a simple resolution providing: "*Resolved,* That during the Eighty-Seventh Congress the Committee on Rules shall be composed of fifteen members." If adopted, this resolution would permit retention of the traditional two-to-one ratio of majority and minority, but the addition of two new "Rayburn men" would ensure an eight-to-seven "liberal" majority even if the Republicans filled all their vacancies and their added spot with conservatives.

In an intense fight, with lobbying by the President, the rest of the Executive Branch, and various interest groups, Rayburn had won the showdown vote, 217 to 212. Thus the Rules Committee, as of the summer of 1961, consisted of the following fifteen members:

DEMOCRATS	REPUBLICANS
HOWARD W. SMITH (Va.), *Chairman*	CLARENCE J. BROWN (Ohio)
WILLIAM M. COLMER (Miss.)	KATHARINE ST. GEORGE (N.Y.)
RAY J. MADDEN (Ind.)	H. ALLEN SMITH (Calif.)
JAMES J. DELANEY (N.Y.)	ELMER J. HOFFMAN (Ill.)
JAMES W. TRIMBLE (Ark.)	WILLIAM H. AVERY (Kans.)
HOMER THORNBERRY (Tex.)	
RICHARD BOLLING (Mo.)	
THOMAS P. O'NEILL, JR. (Mass.)	
CARL ELLIOTT (Ala.)	
B. F. SISK (Calif.)	

On most issues other than civil rights (and some Republican support is usually necessary on this issue to make up for the loss of Southern Democratic votes) the Administration would theoretically be able to count on a paper-thin majority consisting of the eight junior Democrats on the Rules Committee.

But such calculations did not take into account the extremely divisive effects of the religious controversy. The eight-man "Rayburn majority" on

---

* The "twenty-one-day rule" had been tried in 1949–50. It permitted chairmen of standing committees to call up a bill if the Rules Committee delayed more than twenty-one days in providing a special rule.

this committee consisted of three Roman Catholics (Madden, Delaney, and O'Neill), three Methodists from the South (Trimble, Thornberry, and Elliott), one Episcopalian (Bolling), and one member of the Church of Christ (Sisk). With the Administration withholding open support of the parochial-school loan plan and refusing to accept the single-bill tactical approach, would the Catholic members of the committee vote to grant a rule for the public-school bill alone? It was a foregone conclusion that the five Republicans plus Smith and Colmer would oppose granting a rule. And if one or more of the Catholic members insisted on getting a "rule" for the controversial NDEA proposals (as a condition for supporting the public-school bill), would the three Methodist members from the South be willing to go along?

The top strategist for the parochial-school supporters appeared to be House Majority Leader John McCormack. He was reported to have sought assurances that the Administration bill would not be called up for House action before the NDEA amendments (including the parochial-school loan provision) were also ready for floor action. Amid rumors of impending White House intervention and a showdown between Speaker Sam Rayburn (a Primitive Baptist) and John McCormack (a Roman Catholic), the maneuvering continued.

Finally, on June 15 the specific cause of the tie-up became obvious. Rules Committee members O'Neill and Delaney—both Catholics—served notice that they would not vote for a rule for the public-school bill until the NDEA parochial-school provisions were also ready for the floor. The President, back from European conferences with DeGaulle and Khrushchev, got the bad news at his regular Tuesday morning meeting with Congressional leaders. Informally Rayburn was reported to have told Kennedy that the school bill was "as dead as slavery." For the public, however, Rayburn would only indicate that the bill "is in trouble."

On June 20 there was a preliminary showdown in the Rules Committee. Richard Bolling, strategist for the Administration supporters, moved to set a date for Rules Committee hearings on the granting of a "rule" for the public-school bill. A substitute motion that no hearings be held until the parochial-school measure was also before the committee was then advanced. The substitute motion was adopted, 9 to 6, by a majority consisting of the five Republicans, Southern Democrats Smith and Colmer, and Catholics Delaney and O'Neill. The coalition of Republicans and Southern Democrats had often been referred to as an "unholy alliance"; now, as a staff writer for the *Congressional Quarterly* put it, "The 'unholy alliance' has got religion."

Meanwhile the Education and Labor Committee was making slow—and painful—progress on the proposed NDEA changes. Republican members, aware of the log-jam in the Rules Committee, adopted various delaying tactics. It was June 27 before the full committee voted, 19 to 11, to report the measure. Its prospects, however, appeared very poor. Several Republican members of the committee indicated their support for the original NDEA provisions, but they criticized the attempt to make the NDEA amendments the vehicle for authorizing loans to nonpublic schools. To many members of the House the committee bill (H.R. 7904) was perceived simply as the "parochial-school bill."

The final blow to the President's original education proposals came in the Rules Committee on July 18. All three major bills—school aid, NDEA amendments and parochial-school loan, and aid to higher education—were awaiting special rules providing for their floor consideration. But Congressman James Delaney was still not satisfied—a few days earlier he had indicated that all three bills should be killed and a new "nondiscriminatory" measure drafted to permit federal grants to parents of children attending public or nonpublic schools. Within the committee the other two Catholic Democrats, Madden and O'Neill, disagreed, but only one vote was needed to give the old coalition a majority. By an 8-to-7 vote all three bills were set aside. This decision could be reconsidered, but Colmer followed through with an immediate motion to reconsider, which Clarence J. Brown (the ranking Republican) moved to table. This too was adopted, and under committee rules no further motion to reconsider would be in order. As far as the Rules Committee was concerned, the 1961 drive for aid to education was over.

The Administration Tries Again—but Not Very Hard

The next move was up to the President. For the benefit of his White House press conference Kennedy indicated that he was "hopeful" that supporters of his education program "will use those procedures which are available to them under the rules of the House to bring this to a vote and that a majority of the members of Congress will support it." The original proposals, or some substitute measure, could still be brought to the House floor by resorting to one of the extraordinary procedures which would bypass the Rules Committee. Other than unanimous consent (obviously out of the question), there were three such means available, each with its peculiar risks. School-aid supporters could draft a proposed rule providing for consideration, have it referred to the Rules Committee, and then file a discharge petition to force it out. Many House members, however, are opposed to using discharge petitions, even for bills they favor, on the ground that the procedure undermines the committee system. A second means, which seemed even less likely to succeed, would be to pass the bill under "suspension of the rules" procedure—this, however, would require a two-thirds majority of those voting. Finally, the bill might be called up by committee chairman Adam Clayton Powell under the rarely used procedure of "calendar Wednesday"—this would require only a majority vote.

The House customarily dispenses with calendar Wednesday, but a demand for it by one-third of the House members is sufficient to require its use. It provides for a roll call of the legislative committees in alphabetical order. The chairman of a committee that is called upon may, without a special rule, request the consideration of any bill previously reported out by his committee. On paper, calendar Wednesday looks as easy as operating under a special rule; however, in practice members often complicate it by resorting to parliamentary obstruction, repeated quorum calls, and other unusual tactics. But these informal hazards seemed less formidable than the formal complications involved in a discharge petition or suspension of the rules.

Granted that a procedural loophole was available, there was still a major political problem in determining what sort of measure might pass. When HEW Secretary Ribicoff sounded out Congressional sentiments on a possible compromise, he found little enthusiasm. Senators were opposed to settling for what Hubert Humphrey called "a patchwork that would please no one"; they preferred to try for a broad bill in the next session. Speaker Sam Rayburn and most school-aid leaders in the House were dubious that any general aid bill could pass that body. But the President, reluctant to draw a complete blank in the education field, requested one more effort at a watered-down compromise. Aid for teacher salaries would be dropped, but a one-year "emergency" program of $325 million for classroom construction in overcrowded school districts would be linked to extension of the impacted-areas program and the college-student-loan provisions of the NDEA. This package, which appealed to almost no one, was introduced by Congressman Frank Thompson, and became H.R. 8890. School-aid supporters planned to bring it to the floor via calendar Wednesday procedure. A new aid-to-higher-education bill, H.R. 8900, was also made ready.

The compromise school bill was rushed through the Education and Labor Committee, over Republican protests, with discussion limited to seventy minutes. Spokesmen for the NEA repudiated it; opponents of federal aid— sensing victory—attacked it; liberal Republicans, who had supported the move to expand the Rules Committee, criticized the resort to such unusual procedure. On the next Wednesday, August 30, school-aid supporters planned to call the measure up under calendar Wednesday business.

When the clerk began the call of committees no other chairman sought to use the day and thereby delay a showdown. When the Committee on Education and Labor was called, Congressman Powell rose and asked for consideration of H.R. 8890. Congressman Hébert, a Louisiana Democrat, then called for the yeas and nays on the question of consideration (which is nondebatable). The roll call was a lopsided defeat for the Administration. The count was 242 opposed to even considering the bill, 170 in favor. Most non-Southern Democrats (including Catholic members such as Delaney) voted for consideration, but there were only 21 Southern Democrats and a mere 6 Republicans voting "yea." The massive opposition consisted of 160 Republicans, 70 Southern Democrats, and only 12 non-Southern Democrats.

That settled the matter for 1961, but the President was yet to suffer insult added to injury. The problem of renewing the impacted-areas program and the existing NDEA provisions was still unsettled. The Administration wanted a one-year renewal, so that a package education bill could be tried again in 1962. But Minority Leader Charles Halleck (Republican of Indiana) pressed the House Democratic leadership for a two-year extension. This proposal sailed through the House, under "suspension of the rules," by 378 to 32. Meanwhile Judge Smith indicated that he had no immediate plans for granting a rule for the less controversial bill for aid to higher education.

In the Senate the President's supporters made a final attempt to limit the extension of existing programs to one year. But the Senate balked, by a vote of 45 to 40 (the President's plea was heeded by only one Southern Democrat—Kefauver—and only five Republicans). The two-year extension (S. 2393) was then passed, and the Senate bill cleared by the House. It gave the President none of the major provisions he had requested, and it continued for two years those programs he had wanted extended for only one year. When the President, "with extreme reluctance," signed the measure (which became Public Law 87–344) it was no festive occasion; no school-aid supporters came forward to claim the ceremonial pen.

Congress and Aid to Higher Education: The 1962 Story

When Congress adjourned in September 1961 a new school year was beginning. Enrollments were, as usual, setting a new record. But not even the specter of the "classroom gap" could lend sufficient impetus to prospects for a general federal-aid program. The bitterness of the 1961 legislative struggle and the degree of religious antagonism it set loose seemed to indicate that school aid of the sort proposed by President Kennedy was dead, not just for the Eighty-Seventh Congress, but probably for the decade of the 1960's. It remained to be seen whether the antagonisms of the school-aid fight would carry over into the increasingly important field of federal support for higher education.

Issues and Interest Groups: Aid to Higher Education?

Federal involvement in higher education has proceeded along a broad front. Federal assistance has been greatest for the support of advanced research, next greatest for the construction of certain types of physical facilities, and least available for assistance to undergraduates. Graduate and postgraduate research in many fields is financed on contract to the armed services, the Atomic Energy Commission, and the National Aeronautics

NSF

Lou's
fellowship

and Space Agency. Pure science is supported by the National Science Foundation, and medical research has been embarrassingly well provided for by the funds available to the National Institutes of Health and its nine major specialized institutes (each oriented around a major disease area). Passage of the 1958 NDEA program even provided a few graduate fellowships in the neglected area of the humanities and authorized a loan program for undergraduates. The Senate had voted for a federally supported undergraduate scholarship program, but this was strongly opposed by a majority of the House. Students, like migrant farm workers, may have their social needs, but they are politically unorganized and probably unorganizable.

Differences of interest with regard to higher education exist along two major axes. Where special categories of assistance are at issue there is competition between the various disciplines and professions. The "national interest" is considered furthered by some through a special program for training engineers and scientists, by others through assistance to medical and dental schools and students, by others through the training of more and better foreign-language specialists, and by still others through the improvement of the caliber of teachers, and so forth. Where discussion is of across-the-board assistance to institutions or to students, there are differences of interest between various types of colleges and universities. Rapidly growing junior colleges and community colleges feel that they have needs that Harvard and Yale do not have, and established but less prestigious institutions fear that unrestricted scholarships (not tied to attendance within a state) would tend to drain local talent off to the Ivy League or other prestige schools.

Swarthmore!

The interest groups involved in higher education lack the mass membership base of many of the school-aid antagonists, but they have some advantages of higher status and greater prestige. In the discussion of alleged shortages of various specialists and professions the major professional associations are quick to make their voices heard. On questions of more general aid the colleges and universities are organized into a variety of associations. The American Council on Education (ACE) is the largest and best established, but there are a variety of others: the Association of State Universities and Land Grant Colleges, the Association of American Colleges, the American Association of Junior Colleges, and the State Universities Association.

While the students may not realize it, the world of higher education has become increasingly involved in the drive for federal aid, foundation grants, federal research contracts, and other sources of funds. Most institutions of higher education find themselves caught up in a desperate race to keep pace with applications for admission and at the same time to participate in the general "leveling up" process that is going on. As an economist, Adam Smith would hardly be surprised—though as a professor of moral philosophy he might be a bit disturbed—at the speed with which most colleges and universities respond to the incentive of financial support. As HEW Secretary Abraham Ribicoff noted in 1961:

> Federal funds now flow to institutions of higher education for purposes ranging from the building of dormitories to the construction of high-energy accelerators, from research into possible cures for cancer to research into better ways of teaching French, from the training of specialists in nuclear medicine to the education of college teachers of English.

The House Acts—by a Bipartisan Majority

A number of steps were taken before the 1961 adjournment to prepare the way for early 1962 Congressional action on aid to higher education. House hearings on the bill had been held, as mentioned earlier, by Congresswoman Green's subcommittee back in March. In the Senate hearings on aid to higher education (S. 1241 was the Administration bill) were scheduled for August 17, 1961, and continued on August 18 and 21. Senator Morse, the subcommittee chairman, complained that requests for unanimous consent to permit the committee to meet while the Senate was in session had been blocked by Republican Senators, although such requests were being granted for other committees. Once launched, the hearings proceeded expeditiously and with a minimum of controversy.

In the House, a revised higher-education bill, minus the controversial provisions for undergraduate scholarships, had been reported out at the same time as the ill-fated calendar Wednesday school bill. Within the strife-ridden Education and Labor Committee, Chairman Powell had named a special bipartisan "advisory group on higher education." The group had consisted of three young Democrats and two young Republicans, none of whom were major factional figures within the committee and all of whom were sincerely interested in developing a workable bill for aid to higher education. The chairman of the group, who like three of the other four members was only in his second term, was John Brademas (Democrat of Indiana), a onetime Rhodes Scholar and former college professor.

The ostensible task of the "advisory group" was to identify those unmet needs of higher education that most directly affected national security and economic growth. To lend added weight to their research, Brademas and three of his four colleagues made arrangements to visit the Soviet Union and study their system of higher education—one of many so-called Congressional "junkets" undertaken after adjournment. To the amazement of some observers the five-man "advisory group" came up with a series of unanimous recommendations. These called for expanded training of semiprofessional technicians, a program of grants and loans for construction of academic facilities, expansion of the NDEA graduate fellowship program, ← LMB and expansion of the NDEA loan program, including a provision permitting individual institutions to make some outright grants for exceptionally needy undergraduates.

With hardly a hint of controversy in the air the way seemed clear for bipartisan action on a bill for higher education. After a January 16 meeting at the White House, Democratic Congressional leaders indicated that they would press for early action. At a Rules Committee meeting on January 24 a rule (H.R. 527) was granted for the higher-education bill, which was never obtained for the school-aid bill. This vital piece of paper read as follows:

> *Resolved,* That upon the adoption of this resolution it shall be in order to move that the House resolve itself into the Committee of the Whole House on the State of the Union for the consideration of the bill (H.R. 8900) to authorize assistance to public and other nonprofit institutions of higher education in financing the construction, rehabilitation or improvement of needed academic and related facilities, and to authorize financial assistance for undergraduate study in such institutions, and for other purposes, and all points of order against said bill are hereby waived. After general debate, which shall be confined to the bill and continue not to exceed two hours, to be equally divided and controlled by the chairman and ranking minority member of the Committee on Education and Labor, the bill shall be read for amendment under the five-minute rule. At the conclusion of the consideration of the bill for amendment, the Committee shall rise and report the bill to the House with such amendments as may have been adopted and the previous question shall be considered as ordered on the bill and amendments thereto to final passage without intervening motion except one motion to recommit.

With the special rule thus granted, the House "leadership" (which, after the death of Sam Rayburn, consisted of Speaker McCormack and new Majority Leader Carl Albert) scheduled the bill for floor action on January 30. Congressman Ray Madden, from the Rules Committee, called up the resolution providing for consideration. It was routinely adopted. (The time allotted for discussion of a special rule is generally used to discuss the pending substantive measure itself.) The bill's managers, at the urging of Judge Smith, indicated that they would offer a committee amendment to provide that all funds to be obtained under the measure would come via the normal appropriations route, and not through resort to "back-door financing" (a controversial procedure whereby loan programs are authorized to borrow from the U.S. Treasury, thereby circumventing the usual checks on the President via the Congressional appropriations process).

When the House resolved itself into the Committee of the Whole, Homer Thornberry (Democrat of Texas) moved to the rostrum to replace the Speaker as presiding officer. Since the bill had substantial bipartisan support, much of the time was spent in explaining and defending its specific provisions. The spirit of general agreement and lack of acrimony must have been something of a surprise to ex-Congressman Graham Barden, former chairman of the continually wrangling Education and Labor Committee, who was present in the chamber for the debate.

Republican Charles Goodell, an upstate New York member of the "advisory group," summarized the situation in the debate as follows:

> Mr. Chairman, as a very vigorous opponent of general Federal aid-to-education measures, may I at the outset express my strong endorsement of this legislation. . . .
> This is in my opinion a bipartisan bill. . . .
> Getting back to the bipartisan approach, may I simply raise a red flag of warning: This bill includes aid only for academic facilities. . . . If it comes back here from the conference with student assistance in it I think it would jeopardize and probably defeat this bill.

When Congresswoman Green urged that similar bipartisan support was needed for a general school-aid bill, Peter Frelinghuysen replied: "I can assure the gentlewoman I can imagine no bipartisan support for the bill that was advocated by the administration last year." After adoption of the committee amendments, mostly technical, the Committee of the Whole rose and reported the bill back to the House. With the Speaker back in the chair the yeas and nays were ordered. The bill passed by a resounding 319 to 79, with even Judge Smith voting for passage! Opposition was restricted to very conservative Republicans and a limited number of Southern Democrats, some of whom had expressed concern over the church-state implications of a college grant program.

The Senate Concurs—but Differences Remain

The next step was up to the Senate, where enthusiasm for scholarships was stronger and where opposition to grants for nonpublic colleges was firmer. The Senate leadership lost no time in bringing up its version of the higher-education bill. In line with the Administration's original request, it called for loans, rather than grants, for construction and included undergraduate scholarships.

These had been the two main issues discussed in the hearings the previous summer: Should aid for academic facilities be in the form of loans only or of both loans and grants? And should aid for undergraduates be in the form of loans only or of loans plus some scholarships? Virtually everyone had agreed that loans were adequate for building dormitories (which produce revenue) and that fellowships were essential for graduate and postgraduate students. Senator Goldwater had been critical of the range of graduate fellowships already being provided under the 1958 NDEA program, saying that he could not relate "the study of folklore, music, Buddhist studies to our national defense education needs." But the main emerging issues were of aid for academic facilities (which do not produce revenue) and assistance for undergraduates.

In the 1961 hearings spokesmen for higher education had been virtually unanimous in emphasizing the need for some grants, as well as loans for academic facilities. Many public universities and some state governments are prohibited, either by statute or by state constitutions, from borrowing. Private-college spokesmen were likewise unenthusiastic about loans; they could hardly borrow federal funds which they would not have any foreseeable income to repay. Indeed, some spokesmen suggested that such loans would make private fund-raising more difficult: potential donors would be less likely to contribute toward retiring a loan on an aging building than toward building an exciting new structure.

The chief advantage of a loan program was political. A meaningful program for higher education would have to include nonpublic colleges and universities, which account for over 40 per cent of all students. A program of grants including Southern Methodist University as well as Notre Dame would inevitably raise the touchy church-state issue. But for over a decade, federal loans estimated at $1.5 billion had been going to both public and private colleges for dormitories. Hence a loan program had precedent. The complications that would be raised if a bill attempted to provide grants for church-related institutions that were primarily educational but not for those that were primarily religious had been indicated in testimony from a spokesman for the American Civil Liberties Union. He had suggested three criteria: (1) whether or not students and faculty are required to be adherents of the religious group maintaining the institution, (2) whether or not indoctrination in the tenets of the particular faith is a required part of the curriculum, and (3) whether or not the instructional program is committed to those charged with educational responsibility rather than to outside ecclesiastical administrators. These were intellectually interesting distinctions, but Senators shuddered at the thought of having to debate, administer, or interpret them.

Discussion of the scholarship issue had been more down to earth. Some union spokesmen and some conservatives carried over into the discussion of scholarships attitudes that they had developed in thinking about welfare legislation. Union men wandered off into attacks on the "means test," while conservatives indulged in perorations in praise of "initiative" and "self-reliance." But even for those generally in favor of scholarships—and this included a majority of the committee—there were problems. The Administration bill had provided for state scholarship commissions, which would mean a new layer of administrators in most states. How would Negro students fare with such commissions in the South? Might it not be better to leave the administration of scholarships in the hands of the individual institutions, which have experience in the field? How would a scholarship program, if adopted, be fitted in with the existing NDEA loan program? *female*

And there had been other interesting but less tangible problems. Thus *problems* one witness, who had served as President of Bennington College, pointed *with loans* out that "young women appear to be more reluctant than men to burden themselves with loan obligations" and that it was "quite reasonable to *here, here!* suppose that they would be unwilling to equip themselves with what amounts to a negative dowry." Senator Yarborough indicated he had discussed this particular problem with students in Texas and had arrived at the following judgment: "Whether that would be serious if a young man were really in love I doubt, but it might be a deterrent to beginning friendships that might lead to marriage later."

By the time the bill reached the Senate floor in February, the main concern was over the church-state angle of construction aid, rather than the male-female complications of scholarships. Moreover, a number of Senators were becoming increasingly irritated over what they regarded as the intransigent irresponsibility of the House. Relations between the two bodies had taken a turn for the worse when the House had adjourned at the conclusion of the 1961 session in a manner that forced the Senate to accept the House version of several conference reports. This institutional rivalry, long held in bounds by the Texas team of Rayburn and Johnson, was soon to be stimulated by the protracted feud between the respective appropriations committees over conference procedure. Senator Morse neatly alluded to the House-Senate differences in the education area in his opening remarks of the debate:

> I need not tell experienced Senators that if we go to conference we should be in the strongest possible position. I do not want the bill weakened on the floor of the Senate if I can prevent it. . . . Therefore I make my plea at the beginning of this debate, that Senators keep in mind the fact that we are going to conference on this subject matter. I would like the Senate conferees to go into conference with the strongest possible position.

In view of Southern concern over the church-state issue, the bill had been reported out of committee without any construction grants, and no floor effort was made to add such a provision. But even the loan program was disturbing to some Southern Democrats, especially Senator Sam Ervin (Democrat of North Carolina), a former justice of the North Carolina State Supreme Court, a Mason, and a member of the Senate Judiciary Committee. Ervin had proposed an amendment that prohibited making loans to any nonpublic institution of higher education. This suggested addition had seemed so damaging to the purposes of the bill that Senators Morse and Hill had tried to tighten up the restrictions on any aid being used for sectarian or religious purposes but to maintain the principle of helping private as well as public institutions. When Ervin suggested that his own amendment "may have had something to do with the inspiration which led to the presentation of the amendment by the Senator from Oregon and the Senator from Alabama," Morse replied: "I plead guilty to that charge."

The Morse-Hill proviso, which was adopted by a voice vote, stated:

> The term "academic facilities" shall not include (a) any facility intended primarily for events for which admission is to be charged to the general public, (b) any facility used or to be used for sectarian instruction or as a place for religious worship, or (c) any facility which (although not a facility described in the preceding clause) is used or to be used primarily in connection with any part of the program of a school or department of divinity. . . .

This was enough to satisfy Senator Hill, who was facing a re-election campaign in Alabama, and Senator Randolph (Democrat of West Virginia), who had also expressed concerned over the church-state implications.

But Senator Ervin was still not satisfied. He pressed for an eventual roll-call vote on his own more sweeping restriction and spoke strongly for its adoption:

> Madam President [Senator Maurine Neuberger was presiding], after I pointed out that the bill is a bald violation of the first amendment, the proponents of the bill advanced the theory that a church-owned or church-controlled college could segregate secular education from religious education. . . .
>
> That is precisely what Justice Rutledge [in the *Everson* case concerning public aid for parochial students' bus transportation] said could not be done. . . .
>
> No Senator should have any trouble reaching a decision as to how he should vote thereon. If a Senator favors giving religious groups access to the Treasury of the United States and permitting them to use tax moneys to finance their activities he ought to vote against my amendment.

This was strong, if not entirely accurate, language. The Ervin amendment was defeated, 72 to 15, but these fifteen members included a majority of the Southern Senators voting. If a program of loans provoked this sort of opposition, then the prospects for federal grants—which the colleges wanted—did not appear so bright after all.

The scholarship issue evoked much less passion. Senator Lausche spoke feelingly against what he regarded as a move that would weaken the moral fiber of the nation's youth:

> In our country have we reached a stage where we say, in effect, that the only way by means of which we can induce our youth to go to institutions

of higher learning is by paying fully their tuition? Is that in accord with what we have known as the willingness of our youth to work their way through?

This appeal to the Horatio Alger tradition was supported by Senator Holland (Democrat of Florida). Other Senators derided the idea that with current costs (which had risen almost 100 per cent over the past decade alone) a youngster could work his way through M.I.T. with a newspaper route. As Senator Muskie (Democrat of Maine) put it:

> Mr. President, I came from a family of modest means. I managed to get through college by working, scholarship aid, and loans. I think I would be willing to make the same sacrifices today that I made too many years ago to want to remember—but I shudder when I look at the cost of education today compared with what I had to pay when I was an undergraduate.
>
> Scholarship aid does not reduce initiative, Mr. President.

By February 6 most Senators had had their say on the higher-education bill (the Republicans would soon be leaving town for the annual Lincoln Day speeches on the hustings). That was also the day chosen by the White House for release of the President's 1962 Message on Education. It repeated, though only for the record, the 1961 request for school aid. In regard to higher education the President expressed no strong preference as between grants or loans, but he plumped strongly for the undergraduate scholarships: "I recommend that the full 5-year assistance to higher education proposal before the Congress, including scholarships for more than 200,000 talented and needy students and cost of education payments to their colleges, be enacted without delay." The extra White House prod, which went on to list a variety of special education programs as well, was hardly needed by the Senate. The measure passed by a roll-call vote of 68 to 17. Most of the opposition came from Senators who had supported the Ervin amendment limiting aid to public institutions. The following Senators were then named to meet with House conferees and attempt to work out a conference report: Democrats Morse, Hill, McNamara, Yarborough, Clark, and Randolph, and Republicans Prouty, Goldwater, and Javits.

The differences between the House and Senate versions were—as is often the case—quite substantial. The House bill included no scholarships and provided that 60 per cent of the $300 million annual authorization for academic facilities be in the form of grants, with the remaining 40 per cent as loans. The Senate bill provided only for loans ($300 million annually) for academic facilities, included undergraduate scholarships, and also included an additional title (not requested by the Administration) authorizing a special $50-million-per-year program of assistance for the construction of public community colleges. In both houses there had been substantial interest in aiding the rapid expansion of local junior or community colleges as a means of lessening the need for undergraduate scholarships, since these schools could be attended by students living at home.

✦ Political Arithmetic: Delay + Deadlock = Defeat

After Senate passage of the bill the next step would be for the House to name its conferees. But here there was another procedural bottleneck: naming conferees for a conference committee requires either unanimous consent or a special rule from the Rules Committee. And the same hurdle is repeated when it comes to getting House consideration of a conference report. Since both the White House and the Senate were pushing for scholarships that a House majority opposed, a snag appeared likely.

At the opening of the House session on February 8 the following short interchange took place:

> Mr. POWELL: Mr. Speaker, I ask unanimous consent to take from the Speaker's table the Bill H.R. 8900 . . . with the Senate amendments thereto, disagree to the Senate amendments, and agree to the conference requested by the Senate.
> THE SPEAKER: Is there objection to the request of the gentleman from New York?
> Mr. QUIE: Mr. Speaker, I object.

The effect of this four-word speech was to toss the measure back into the custody of Judge Smith and the Rules Committee, where a majority of the members were opposed to scholarships.

With the session barely a month old there seemed lots of time for bargaining maneuvers, but time on Capitol Hill is a scarce commodity. The weeks passed, and it was cherry blossom time in Washington before the bill's House managers were willing, or able, to come to terms with Judge Smith and his associates. Finally, at a closed session of the Rules Committee on April 17 the assurances of the bill's backers that they would stand fast in opposition to a scholarship provision were deemed acceptable, and Rules Committee clearance seemed forthcoming. Following the Easter recess the necessary resolution (H.R. 625) was duly voted out, 8 to 6, but it was May 9 before it was brought to the House floor. The resolution provided as follows:

> Resolved, That immediately upon the adoption of this resolution the bill (H.R. 8900) to authorize assistance to public and other nonprofit institutions of higher education in financing the construction, rehabilitation, or improvement of needed academic and related facilities, with the Senate amendments thereto, be, and the same hereby is, taken from the Speaker's table, to the end that the Senate amendments be, and they are hereby, disagreed to and that the conference requested by the Senate on the disagreeing votes of the two Houses be, and the same is hereby, agreed to.

Dear Powell what a stew he's in now

Congressman Powell indicated clearly enough what the price for this procedural clearance had been:

> I have given my word privately to the chairman of the Committee on Rules, I have given my word publicly to the entire Committee on Rules and I give my word now to my colleagues that under no circumstances when we go to conference will we recede from the House position; that we will at all times maintain only those provisions voted by the House.

Powell went on:

> We will come back with a bill without scholarships. If we cannot find a common ground between the two groups of conferees we will come back and so report to you. Again I repeat that under no circumstances will we accept the scholarship provision in conference with the Senate.

On these clearly stated terms even Judge Smith was willing to see the measure go to conference:

> Mr. Speaker, I think there is no controversy about sending this bill to conference; and the conditions under which it is sent have been very frankly stated and have been agreed to both by the members of the Committee on Rules and the members of the Committee on Education and Labor. So I am supporting the rule.

This did not mean, however, that conservatives such as Judge Smith were fully convinced of the wisdom of the act:

> Mr. Speaker, I want to talk about the general situation of Federal aid to education because in all the years I have been here, I do not think I have ever seen anything so completely and hopelessly confused on anything that has come before this Congress as the situation now on Federal aid to education.

And the Judge went on to indicate his concern over duplication of education programs, and the total costs implied by existing and proposed programs (including a bill from the Commerce Committee authorizing assistance for medical and dental colleges).

The resolution was approved by the House on a 295-to-77 roll-call vote. The Speaker then appointed the following House conferees: Democrats Powell, Green, Brademas, and Giaimo, and Republicans Kearns, Quie, and Goodell. But the substantive grounds on which a compromise might be reached were by no means clear. Meanwhile it proved difficult even to get the House and Senate conferees together: Senator Hill was preoccupied with a primary campaign in Alabama, Senator Goldwater had children

showing his true colors

graduating from college, and Congressman Powell was off on another trip outside the country.

But there was worse to come. The Supreme Court's decision of June 25, striking down the use of an official prayer in the public schools, set off a storm of controversy over the role of religion in public education. Meanwhile, the leading organizations in the drive for federal aid for public schools had become alarmed that the college-aid program, whether of grants or of loans, would set a precedent (as the NDEA loan program had) that would be invoked in future school-aid debates. At its annual convention the NEA adopted a resolution against providing grants for nonpublic colleges.

As the summer wore on, it seemed unlikely that the conferees would be able to come up with any sort of compromise. The White House appeared uninterested, and Senator Morse was now engaged in a bitter filibuster against the Administration's "Telstar" satellite bill. Efforts at reaching a conference committee compromise eventually fell to Congresswoman Green, the bill's House sponsor, and to Senator Clark, who had become deeply concerned over higher education while serving on a task force studying the problem in the state of Pennsylvania.

What Congresswoman Green and Senator Clark finally came up with was unlikely to satisfy anyone completely; the crucial question was whether it would prove satisfactory to a majority of the House and Senate. As finally filed, the conference report provided for the following: (1) a program of grants and loans for academic facilities, available to all colleges, but for use only for the construction of science, engineering, and library buildings; (2) undergraduate assistance in the form of loans, but with each institution authorized to make 20 per cent of its loans on a "nonreimbursable" basis; (3) the public-community-college program, with aid narrowed to the same types of facilities as those specified in the general academic-facilities provision. The Senate conferees had voted to approve the compromise, 7 to 2 (Senators Hill and Goldwater dissenting); the House conferees had approved, 6 to 1 (Congressman Kearns dissenting). Hill had objected—strongly—to grants for nonpublic colleges, Goldwater had been opposed to virtually the whole bill, and Kearns had objected to disguising scholarships as "nonreimbursable" loans.

The conference report, which had been informally cleared with the Rules Committee, was filed on September 19. Its prospects did not appear good. The NEA, largest of the public-school-aid groups, launched an all-out attack, flying lobbyists in from out of town and sending telegrams to all members charging that the grant provision "imperils America's traditional concept of separation of church and state." Like Kearns, many Republicans in the House were bitter over the "semantic doubletalk" involved in the term "nonreimbursable" loans. And Senator Hill, although a leading Southern "liberal" who had fathered many health and education bills, was reported to have personally urged the members of the Alabama delegation in the House to oppose the conference report. Senator Hill's concern over the Alabama political climate (tension was mounting as James Meredith's efforts to enter the nearby University of Mississippi moved toward a show-down) was no figment of his imagination. In the November 1962 elections, after trailing his obscure Republican opponent for most of the election night, Hill eked out a bare 51 per cent margin of victory.

On September 20, with the House in a stretch drive for adjournment, Congresswoman Green led off the House floor debate on adoption of the conference report. In a bluntly worded speech she defended the compromise as "a good bill," with concessions made on both the House and Senate sides. She sought to meet the religious question head on, listing grants that had previously gone even to Baptist-related colleges under the NDEA loan pro-gram, or from the Atomic Energy Commission, National Institutes of Health, and National Science Foundation. And she criticized the NEA for its posi-tion:

> May I say to my friends in the education profession—and I say this with a heavy heart—if they are successful in stirring up enough religious controversy on this, I do not think we will see an education bill in the Congress in the foreseeable future. This is a case of cutting off the nose to spite the face.

Congressmen Quie and Goodell, the young Republicans who had served on the "advisory group on higher education" and had signed the conference report, spoke for the compromise. But they could not stem the tide of Re-publican opposition. And Southern Democrats—now fully alarmed over the church-state issue—closed ranks in opposition also. After Adam Clayton Powell gave a somewhat rambling explanation of his role, the crucial motion was made by Carroll Kearns, the ranking Republican member of the Edu-cation and Labor Committee:

> Mr. Kearns moves to recommit the conference report on the bill, H.R. 8900, to the committee of conference with instructions to the managers on the part of the House to insist upon the House position by striking title II of the amendment to H.R. 8900 as reported in the conference report.

In theory the vote would involve only recommiting the bill and would in-dicate House disapproval only of the undergraduate-assistance provision (Title II). In fact, however, there was widespread opposition to the grant and loan program (Title I), and there would be little time remaining for a last-ditch salvage effort.

The yeas and nays were ordered, and the clerk began to call the roll. In the House this requires about thirty minutes. There was no dramatic last-minute appeal from the President; there were no White House liaison men hovering anxiously in the wings. When the roll call was finished the count stood 214 for recommital (and presumably against the bill) and 186 opposed to recommital (and presumably in favor of the bill). The lineup was an almost classic example of the "conservative coalition" at work: the majority consisted of 130 Republicans, 73 Southern Democrats, and 11 other Democrats; the minority consisted of 142 non-Southern Democrats, 30 Republicans, and a mere 14 Southern Democrats.

Preliminary efforts at salvaging Title I alone (the aid for academic facilities) soon proved fruitless. The Eighty-Seventh Congress would honor educational needs by passing a minor bill authorizing aid to educational TV stations; it would even modify the barrier to aid put up by the non-Communist affidavit required by the NDEA bill. But it would go no further; this was the end of the line for the President's proposals for aid to education.

Conclusions and Comments

President Kennedy's problems with Congress over education suggest a variety of comments and interpretations. The agenda of major issues facing the country in the 1960's includes a few that have come into clear focus and can be neatly analyzed as "cases" of decision. But a far greater number, including federal aid for education, are closer to the category of "non-cases." That is to say, they are areas in which repeated efforts by a variety of actors using a number of procedures have been blocked. Such situations may be less dramatic but are more typical of how Congress works.

Presidential Leadership: The Missing Link

It has become customary to look to the President both for bold intellectual leadership in the identification of problems and for strong political leadership in urging Congress toward some response. Why, in this age of Presidential leadership, was the education struggle allowed to become so clear an example of Congressional-style politics? To some observers, President Kennedy's performance seemed more in the tradition of Eisenhower than of FDR. Was the defeat of the Kennedy education proposals due primarily to a faulty initial analysis of the problem, or to failure to provide adequate political follow-through, or was it—given the structure of the situation—an inevitable outcome? Each of these possible interpretations is worth examining for the light it sheds on the powers and limitations of the Presidency and Congress.

To support the first view it can be argued that the President's original education proposals were no bold new look at education needs, but rather a "warmed-over" version of a 1950's bill that had been prompted by a late 1940's education crisis. This proposed legislation, then, contrasted markedly with the innovation involved in the Peace Corps or the amount of care and thought that went into the Trade Expansion Act. It is the Executive Branch that is usually thought of as the source of innovation and Congress that is criticized for thinking in horse-and-buggy terms. But the Administration's original school-aid program reflected little more than the traditional goals of the NEA (which have usually been expressed within government by the Office of Education). It was within Congress that voices were raised over the need for scientific and technical manpower, that enthusiasm was generated for the special potential of the junior college, and that opposition crystallized to the state administration of scholarships. And it was largely owing to Congress that a searching reexamination of the role, aspirations, costs, and expectations of nonpublic schools has been undertaken. If the rethinking involved here is sometimes painful for Catholics and many non-Catholics alike, it is also very much needed.

Not until December 1962 did Presidential policy reflect Congressional demands for revised estimates of traditional educational needs. The President commented as follows:

> Here we are going to have twice as many people trying to go to college in 1970 as 1960. That means we have to build as many buildings in ten years as we built the whole 160 years of our nation's history. Then you have got these millions of young boys and girls who are dropping out of school, who are unskilled, at a time when . . . skilled labor is needed, and not unskilled. So we need money for vocational training to train them in skills, to retrain workers, to provide assistance funds for colleges, and then to provide assistance to those who are going to get doctorates, higher advanced degrees in engineering, science and mathematics. We have a severe shortage there.

This emphasis on selective federal aid for specific areas within education is vastly different from Kennedy's original proposals for across-the-board public-school aid sent to Congress eighteen months earlier.

A second view, common to enthusiastic supporters of the President's original program, emphasizes his failure really to throw his support behind his education program. The White House seemed ever ready to compromise but never ready to fight. As a New York *Times* editorial commented in late 1961: "The story of the school bill's debacle has been a succession of profiles in lack of courage." But this observation only leads to the further question of *why* the President did not battle for his program. Was it because the costs of eventual success appeared too high to warrant the effort, or was it because the prospects appeared hopeless?

The religious issue certainly increased the risks the President would run if he were to make an all-out effort for an education bill. If the logic of legislative politics suggested the need for some sort of compromise on aid for nonpublic schools, the logic of Presidential politics—geared to the potential impact of the public's reaction on the 1964 election—surely suggested avoiding Presidential involvement in any such move. In national

Public Reaction to the President's Aid-to-Education Program:

1) Liberal and pro-Administration commentators stressed public-school needs.

"KEEP YOUR HANDS OFF THAT INNOCENT SCHOOLMARM!"

Mauldin in the St. Louis *Post-Dispatch*

"We Can't Burden Our Children With Deficit Spending"

Herblock in *The Washington Post*

2) Conservatives emphasized the costs and hidden dangers of federal controls.

"This way it's not out of my pocket."

D. Hesse in the St. Louis *Globe-Democrat*

Trojan Horse

D. Hesse, McNaught Syndicate, Inc.

3.) Meanwhile, the issue of aid to parochial schools grew more prominent week by week.

'Help! Help!'

G. Allison Wells in the *Catholic News*

Ed Valtman – *The Hartford* (Conn.) *Times*

4.) When the bills were finally lost in Congress, defeat was seen as the fruit of Presidential tactics.

Crawford, Newspaper Enterprise Association

James J. Dobbins in the Boston *Traveler*

politics a leader often has to lean over backwards to avoid being accused of favoritism. As General Eisenhower went out of his way to avoid appearing to be a militarist, so President Kennedy has faced a problem in living down widespread fears that he would be pro-Catholic. In the speech that opened his 1960 campaign, Kennedy had said that this decade "will demand that the President place himself in the very thick of the fight, that he care passionately about the fate of the people he leads, that he be willing to serve them at the risk of incurring their momentary displeasure." This was certainly not the course that the President had followed in regard to education. But in national politics there are always a number of major issues at stake. The President was simply not prepared to jeopardize his whole legislative program—and perhaps his chances for re-election—by a bitter fight to the death for aid to education. Lacking a popular ground swell in support of the program, the President's chief alternative was to press for some acceptable compromise on aid for nonpublic schools. And this was a move involving great risks for a Catholic President.

Congressman Richard Bolling had once described Judge Smith's political skill as follows:

> But on an economic issue, or a welfare issue, if there are, let's say, five or six of them, he'll play them as carefully as he can and very skillfully to kill as many as possible, but if he has to knuckle under in order to get X by going along with A he will.

The President's legislative problem was, like that of Judge Smith, to get as many victories as possible but to "knuckle under" when necessary. By the end of the 1961 session, the President could count an impressive series of legislative victories, including aid for depressed areas, broadened minimum-wage coverage, and a liberal housing bill. He had fought hard for long-term financing of foreign aid, although he had had to settle for substantially less than he asked for. The Administration had deliberately refrained from endorsing civil-rights legislation in order to facilitate passage of other parts of its program. Similarly, the President apparently decided to knuckle under on aid to education. He could not hope to win every round against the conservative coalition in the House.

This leaves the third possibility—that the situation was simply a lost cause, beyond any hope of redemption. As the President put it in looking back at the 1962 steel-pricing crisis: "There is no sense in raising hell and then not being successful." Politics is the art of the possible, and if the religious issue made agreement on a general school-aid bill impossible, then that was that. But this interpretation does not explain the situation on the higher-education bills, which cleared both House and Senate by heavy margins. After being blocked in the school-aid area, why was the President unable to establish priorities in order to facilitate House-Senate agreement on an academic-facilities bill, and ensure that at least something was accomplished? In dealing with Cuba the President displayed a skill and vigor in 1962 that he had lacked in early 1961; in dealing with education, however, the President made 1962 only a bleak repetition of the failure of 1961.

Congress: Responsible or Obstructionist?

If nothing else, the Congressional response to the Kennedy education program demonstrates in a dramatic way that Congress continues to be a major factor in American government. Indeed, after almost two years in the White House, President Kennedy found himself newly impressed with the power of Congress:

> I think the Congress looks more powerful sitting here than it did when I was there in the Congress. But that is because when you are in Congress you are one of a hundred in the Senate or one of 435 in the House, so that the power is so divided. But from here I look at a Congress, and I look at the collective power of the Congress, particularly the bloc action, and it is a substantial power.

Granted that Congress still has substantial power, is it used responsibly? Evaluation here is all too prone to be a matter of partisanship. The mere fact that Congress fails to approve a given Presidential proposal is not in itself an indictment of Congress; the whole purpose of representative government is to provide an effective check against measures that the Executive feels will be good for the people. Nor is Congress an appendage of the Government Printing Office, to be evaluated by the sheer number of bills and resolutions it cranks out. Just as the Presidency is basically a political office, so Congress is essentially a political institution. And it is best understood in terms of such political functions as providing representation for strongly held views and affording opportunities for arriving at compromise.

The twin functions of representation and consensus formation are not easily reconciled. The complex procedures and multiple hurdles of the legislative process ensure that action will not be taken often in the absence of at least substantial agreement. This reality tends to favor the status quo since when everyone disagrees, inaction is the simple—and sometimes inevitable—solution. Thus a minority that strongly wants something done by the government is in a much weaker tactical position than a minority that is opposed to such action. In dealing with education Congress seems to have represented the conflicting points of view quite adequately; it was in providing a means for compromise that Congress, and especially the House, performed less adequately.

We are used to noting the difference in constituency between the President and Congress, but there are also some fascinating contrasts within Congress between the House and Senate. Senators, representing large, diverse constituencies with at least some urban concentrations and serving long terms, found compromise on education relatively easy (so long as segregation was not directly at issue). Except in the year or two immediately preceding a reelection campaign, most Senators can afford to be "statesmen" even to the point of voting against apparent constituency wishes on at least some issues. On education, as on many issues, the Senate tended toward a more "liberal" or more nearly "Presidential" view than did the House.

Most House members, by contrast, represent small districts, which are often relatively homogeneous (compare a Senator from the *state* of New York with a House member from Brooklyn or from rural, upstate New York!). Also, by the time major legislation reaches the floor of the House the next campaign is never much more than a year away. On many issues the House thus represents a variety of extremes (somewhat like a European multiparty system), but with a conservative bias resulting from the workings of the seniority system and rural-biased state apportionment of districts. Only a few representatives, usually from districts that are both diverse and relatively "safe" (like Richard Bolling's Kansas City district: a microcosm of downtown, stockyards, and suburbia), can afford to play the "statesman" role (however they define it) with any degree of safety.

On the explosive parochial-school issue, compromise was accomplished *within* most Senators themselves, but would have to be negotiated *between* members in the House. In the latter body there were many Catholic members from overwhelmingly Catholic districts, and, on the other hand, many rural Republicans and Southern Democrats from districts where a priest is seldom seen. In the Senate, however, almost every Senator (except those from some Southern states plus Utah and Idaho) had a considerable Catholic minority to consider. (Only Rhode Island has a clear state-wide Catholic majority; Massachusetts is about half and half.) Hence most Senators approached the religious issue very gingerly. The House with its larger percentage of Catholic members (88 out of 437, as compared to 12 out of 100 in the Senate) was "more representative" but less prone to reach some kind of consensus.

Those who are defeated under the existing scheme of things often argue the need for "a change in the rules." But, as Mark Twain said about the weather, the rules are easier to talk about than to do something about. The existence of the seniority system, the power of the Rules Committee in the House, and the possibility of unlimited debate in the Senate all have major political consequences. But the education program was lost more from lack of political skill and support than because of the rules themselves. When the House Rules Committee blocks a bill, it may be frustrating the will of the majority of the members (though it could hardly afford to do this often), but, on the other hand, it may be taking the criticism for doing precisely what a majority want it to do. The events of 1961 rather clearly indicate that in regard to education the latter was the case. When Congressman Delaney blocked further action he was much criticized in the press, but to many of his colleagues he was something of a hero—in the absence of a proposal that a majority could accept, he was absorbing the criticism on a divisive issue that most members preferred to avoid. This tactic may not be entirely laudable, but it is certainly understandable.

Interest Groups and Representation

Neither Congress nor the President works in a political vacuum. Both are much concerned with the view of the organized groups and associations that are involved in a given activity such as education. Thus both the National Education Association and the National Catholic Welfare Council have other primary concerns, but on educational policy they are perceived as "interest groups" with a legitimate concern over the pattern of government policy in education. If such groups did not indicate how legislation would affect them and how they felt about proposed measures, it would be almost impossible for Congressmen to deal intelligently with any problem. Indeed, this information function is the ultimate constitutional basis for the power of Congress to investigate and even compel witnesses to testify at hearings.

Major interest groups have their own political problems, both internal and external. Success in affecting public policy depends upon the extent to which a general coalition of related groups can be put together (within the broad world of "education" or of "agriculture") and the amount of direct opposition by an opposing coalition (as in the case of management versus labor). In the case of education the direct opposition, such as the National Association of Manufacturers and the Chamber of Commerce, was in a relatively weak position and doubtless would have been unable to halt a bill that had the solid backing of the NEA, the higher-education associations, and spokesmen for the nonpublic schools. The difficulty was that there was no such coalition; the conflicting voices of public-school supporters, parochial-school supporters, and various higher-education supporters canceled each other out. The baffled politician might well ask: "Who speaks for education?"

Coalition formation among the various education groups was complicated by lack of communication. Just as Congressmen need to know what various groups want and, in a crude sense, how strongly they want it, so the various groups need to adjust their individual priorities in view of the priorities of other groups. At least part of the failure of the educational community to achieve any of its positive goals was due to poor communication. Would the NEA have pushed as strongly for salary aid if they had realized how much this would upset parochial-school leaders? Would Catholic spokesmen have advanced claims for equal assistance for parochial-school students if they had realized how strongly this would upset many non-Catholics? Would higher-education spokesmen have pushed as vigorously for grants rather than loans if they had perceived the full delicacy of the church-state issue? Or were the "leaders" in some measure the captives of their followers on these issues? After all, a Prohibition party can hardly afford to compromise on the issue of liquor, and the NEA (to cite one example) might have found it equally difficult to compromise on teacher salaries. The goals and even the tactics of an organization are often sharply limited by its need to provide effective inducements to assure the continued support of its members.

Aid to Education: Was There a Decision?

Some decisions are made in the form of dramatic showdowns; others seem to be arrived at almost unconsciously and can be fully perceived only in retrospect. Defeat of the Kennedy education program in the Eighty-Seventh Congress did not mean that no decisions were reached or that the matter was just postponed with the same agenda and the same issues to be faced another day. In retrospect it appeared that the drive for across-the-board public-school aid, of the sort desired by the NEA and the American Federation of Teachers, was now dead. Indeed, the last real chance to pass such a measure may have been in the wake of the Soviet *sputnik,* which was launched in the fall of 1957. Had the *sputnik* come a year earlier, before President Eisenhower became so alarmed over the budget, it might have resulted in passage of a school-aid bill. Or if it had come a year later, after the Democratic Congressional sweep of 1958, it might have helped produce such a bill.

In the 1950's federal policy toward education was at a fork in the road. To the right was the path of minimum federal involvement; to the left was the path of massive federal aid with a minimum of federal control. This, with overtones of race and religion, was what the debates of 1950–60 were about. But in fact there was a third path, not clearly discerned and not much debated, to which the federal government seems increasingly committed. This is a pattern of selective federal involvement, based on a wide variety of special-category aid programs. Thus we already have federal aid for impacted areas; for hot school lunches; for improved teaching of mathematics, science, and foreign languages; for graduate fellowships; for scientific research; for medical research; and for vocational training. This pattern seems likely to grow.

The agenda for future education debates may turn, not on the need for general school aid (except perhaps as a depression measure), but on the relative priorities of various special-category problems. What, if anything, is to be done to aid junior colleges, to assist medical and dental schools (and students), to upgrade the skills of unemployed workers, to help finance college academic facilities, or to deal with high school "dropouts"? Should more of the country's talent be steered into medicine or into mathematics, into nursing or into nuclear physics?

If this is the direction in which Congressional debate and government policy do move, it will involve some interesting paradoxes. The symbol of "federal aid" was defeated, but federal involvement in education already amounts to $2 billion per year and continues to grow. Everyone favors an efficient, responsible pattern of administration, but the programs are scattered among dozens of government agencies rather than concentrated in one, and they often involve education only as a sort of sideline (as with the Atomic Energy Commission or the National Aeronautics and Space Agency). Almost no one favors federal "control," but the emerging pattern of specialized assistance virtually ensures a substantial degree of federal influence. If nothing else, the mere allocation of federal funds to some programs and not to others will—as is intended—exert tremendous leverage on the over-all structure of American education.

Just as war is too important to be left entirely up to the generals, so education is too important to be left entirely up to the school administrators. The latter are not only involved as participants in the politics of education but by now have received something of an education in politics.

What of
CIA + NSA ??

religious issue
loan vs. scholarship
segregation

3

Bookies and "Bugs" in California

Judicial Control of Police Practices

Alan F. Westin

CRIMINAL trials hold an unending fascination for most Americans, and for many of the same reasons that people flocked to see trial by combat in Norman England or witches hanged at Salem. At its rational best, the courtroom is a superb snapshot of the human condition and its byways: the prosecutor's quest for punishment in the name of "the People," the defense counsel's wall of sheltering objections around his client, the stream of witnesses dropping bits and pieces of "the Truth," the defendant's outraged innocence or brotherly plea of justification, the mixture of community passions and pity called a jury, and the ambiguous presence of the judge as participant-referee. Criminal trials are also the setting for passionate debates over bedrock principles of American democracy—from police practices and the definition of crimes against state and nation to the conditions of fair trial and appeal. These debates will often widen into celebrated arguments over constitutional history, the standards of judicial review, and the line between judicial and political functions. From their start in a local police court or federal courthouse, such trials can run a judicial gantlet which, if survived, leads to the cavernous majesty of the courtroom of the United States Supreme Court.

LONG BEACH—California's fifth largest city, with 350,000 residents—lies seventeen miles due south of downtown Los Angeles. Its eight and one-half miles of broad white beachfront along the Pacific Ocean make it a resort playground for the Angelenos and Southern Californians generally.

One of the restaurants in Long Beach that Duncan Hines did not recommend in the 1950's was the Red Onion Café, at 123 American Avenue, nestled among several thriving bars. On April 1, 1952, its owner, Patrick Irvine, a usually genial fifty-year-old Irish-American, was seated beside an officer in Superior Court of the State of California in and for the County of Los Angeles, Department of Long Beach, charged with violating Section 337a of the California Penal Code. Sanitary conditions at the Red Onion Café were not at issue, for restaurateur Patrick Irvine was in court that morning in his capacity as one of Long Beach's leading bookmakers.

California, home of such celebrated race tracks as Santa Anita, Hollywood Park, and Tanforan, permits betting on horse races only at the pari-mutuel windows at the tracks themselves (where the state skims off a rich percentage of the betting pools in taxes). Section 337a of the California Penal Code makes it a crime for anyone other than the track ticket-sellers to:

1. engage in pool-selling or bookmaking;
2. keep . . . any room, shed, tenement, tent, booth, building, float, vessel, place, stand or inclosure . . . with a book or books, paper or papers, apparatus, device or paraphernalia, for the purpose of recording or registering any bet . . . or wager upon the result . . . of any trial . . . or contest of skill, speed or power of endurance of man or beast . . . or mechanical apparatus . . . or upon the result . . . of any lot, chance, casualty, unknown or contingent event . . . ; [or]
3. [hold] any money, thing or consideration of value, or the equivalent or memorandum thereof, staked, pledged, bet or wagered . . . upon the result [of such contests].

Violation of Section 337a is punishable by thirty days to one year in the county jail or a year in the state penitentiary at the judge's discretion.

On the evening of January 5, 1952, Patrick Irvine and his wife, Mildred, were in the living room of their home at 3916 East Second Street. At 7 P.M., Detective Inspector Everett Kennedy of the bookmaking detail of the Long Beach police department opened the front door of the Irvine house with a specially made key. Accompanied by a police sergeant, he walked into the living room and announced, "Pat, this is an arrest." Irvine's dog began to bark angrily at the inspector and had to be tied up in the kitchen. A half-hour later, three newspaper photographers arrived to take pictures of the arrest and to follow Irvine down to the police station to record his "booking." Thus was completed the first formal step in the case of *The People of the State of California* v. *Patrick Irvine, Morris Jamoke Lippe, and Pete Emil Curti.*

In most states, criminal prosecutions are initiated by having an indictment voted by a grand jury. In others, such as California, prosecutions may be initiated by the district attorney filing a verified complaint in Municipal Court charging a defendant with committing a crime. A preliminary hearing is then held before a magistrate who decides whether there is "probable cause" to place the accused on trial. If probable cause is found, defendant is held in custody (or released on bail). An "information" is then filed by the district attorney in Superior Court and the trial is thereby launched. Probable cause was found in the case of Irvine and his two employees, and the district attorney of Los Angeles County filed an information on February 13, 1952, charging five counts of felony:

Count 1 charged Irvine, Lippe, and Curti with conspiracy to violate Section 337a. It was charged, as one of several "overt acts" proving this conspiracy, that the three men had purchased federal wagering-tax stamps.

Count 2 charged the defendants with "wilfully, unlawfully, and feloniously engaging in poolselling and bookmaking."

Count 3 charged them with the keeping of premises at 10851 South Chestnut Street, Los Alamitos, and 3916 East Second Street, Long Beach, with paraphernalia for recording and registering bets on horse races.

Count 4 charged them with receiving money and memoranda thereof for wagering on horse races.

Count 5 charged them with the recording and registering of bets on horse races.

On March 3, Irvine, Lippe, and Curti each pleaded not guilty as charged on each count of the information and demanded trial by jury.

Pat and the "Mike"—Trial in Superior Court

Irvine's trial opened on April 1, 1952, three months after his arrest, in Superior Court for Los Angeles County, Department E of Long Beach, Judge Ralph K. Pierson presiding. Each of California's fifty-eight counties has a Superior Court. In large counties with heavy case loads, this Superior Court is divided into departments, Los Angeles having 120 departments at the present time. The judges are elected on a county-wide nonpartisan ballot for six-year terms.

On April 3, after the jury had been chosen and the clerk had read the information, the veteran deputy district attorney for Los Angeles County, Thomas W. Cochran, rose to deliver his opening statement.

The People would show, Cochran said, that Irvine and his two employees, Lippe and Curti, had conspired to engage in and had engaged in bookmaking activities at Irvine's home and at a second location, 10851 South Chestnut Street in nearby Los Alamitos. The evidence of these activities would be of several types. First, there would be proof that Irvine, Lippe, and Curti had each applied for and secured a $50 wagering stamp from the tax division of the federal Internal Revenue Bureau. (In 1951, as a result of Senator Estes Kefauver's dramatic hearings on organized crime, Congress had passed an act requiring all persons receiving wagers to apply for a license stamp, pay a $50 fee, list their place of business, and pay a 10 per cent special tax on all amounts wagered with them. Failure to obtain the stamp and pay the tax is punishable by a fine of $1,000 to $5,000. Congress was quite aware that state and local police would hurry to see who applied and where they were doing business. Indeed, the legislation specified that payment of the tax and fee would *not* bar state prosecutions for wagering or give any immunity to those registering, and the applications were made public records open for inspection.)

Second, Cochran continued, the People would introduce recorded conversations and summaries of conversations overheard among Irvine, Lippe, Curti, and Mildred Irvine proving that bookmaking was being carried on at Irvine's home and over his telephone. Cochran described how these conversations were secured and gave samples of what the talks contained.

Third, the People would prove that Curti and a woman named Audie Greer had taken betting records from the South Chestnut Street house and had delivered them by car to Irvine's home. That fact would be shown on the basis of a police trap by which, on January 5, the papers being carried by Curti and Audie Greer were impregnated with a fluorescent powder visible only under a fluoroscope. Traces of the powder were found, Cochran explained, on Irvine's hands and on bookmaking records in his bedroom desk at the time of his arrest on January 5.

Cochran instructed the jurors that his description of these facts and events, being an opening statement for the prosecution, "was not evidence." That would have to "come from the witnesses." It was only a general, chronological narrative of "what I believe and expect that the evidence in this case will prove."

The attorney for Irvine, Lippe, and Curti was Andrew H. McConnell of Long Beach, a former Montana criminal prosecutor who became a defendant's attorney. This was not the first time that McConnell had been Irvine's counsel. "As a criminal lawyer," he recalled, "I had represented

Irvine and his brother Joe, and many of their employees, for a number of years on charges of violation of the [liquor] prohibition laws, and later of the horse-racing laws of this State."

Following Cochran's opening statement to the jury for the People, Mc-Connell would ordinarily have made a comparable statement for the defense. He chose to waive that right, however, and Judge Pierson directed the People to put on its witnesses.

Enter Russell Mason, the Happy Wirer

Cochran called as his initial witness a man who was to be perhaps the second most important figure in the case, Russell Dean Mason. His special connection with the investigation was quickly developed by the questioning:

> Mr. Cochran: Mr. Mason, what is your business or occupation?
> Mr. Mason: Recording engineer.
> Mr. Cochran: Will you tell the jury just briefly, please, what a recording engineer is?
> Mr. Mason: A person that makes it their [sic] business to use recording equipment to record voices, sounds, or any types of noises, picked up from a microphone and run through various amplifiers and so forth, into a recording machine. . . .
> Mr. Cochran: How long have you been engaged in that work, Mr. Mason?
> Mr. Mason: Since 1928.
> Mr. Cochran: Have you devoted practically your entire time to the work of a recording engineer since that time?
> Mr. Mason: Since about the last 10 or 15 years exclusively in that type of work.

Cochran then brought out by his questioning that Mason had done such recordings previously for the district attorney's office of Los Angeles County and had appeared in California and federal courts as "an expert on recording devices." Mason then explained the electronic-eavesdropping or "bugging" process by which sounds in a room (including human voices) are picked up by a sensitive microphone and transmitted by wire to a listening post where the sounds can be heard through earphones or recorded automatically on magnetic tape.

Having qualified Mason as an expert and described the eavesdropping process, Cochran was now ready to let Mason tell his story.

> Mr. Cochran: Tell the jury what you did on December 3rd.
> Mr. Mason: On December 3rd, it was during the evening, I took my truck and drove down to this address, parked in the alley, took off one of my ladders [from] the truck and carried the wire that I had strung up previously up to the roof of . . . 3916 East Second, which is composed of some garages with living quarters up above. And I bored a hole

> in the roof, stuck my wire through the roof. I came downstairs [into Irvine's house] . . . crawled up into a little hole in the closet and installed a microphone above the light in the fixture box. . . . Then I went back to the place we term as the listening post . . . I connected up the equipment, connected the wire to the preamplifier, connected the preamplifier to the recording equipment, and turned it on "on" position.

Mason continued this part of his account by noting that he made several tests (with officers talking from Irvine's house), that he instructed the police officers at the listening post in the proper operation of the equipment, and that he then left in his truck with his wife, who had come along to aid him in secreting the microphone.

Tapping, Bugging, and the Law

At this point, we must pause to summarize the legal rules affecting Mason's activities as a police eavesdropper. Since the United States is a federal system, both federal and state governments have their own court systems where criminals are tried and rules of evidence are adopted to govern the conduct of these trials. Unless the Supreme Court of the United States holds that a provision of the federal Constitution limits the jurisdiction of the states, each state is free to set its own rules of evidence and courtroom procedure.

The Fourth Amendment to the federal Constitution, adopted in 1791 as part of the Bill of Rights limiting federal power, deals with search-and-seizure matters. It provides that:

> The right of the people to be secure in their persons, houses, papers, and effects, against unreasonable searches and seizures, shall not be violated, and no warrants shall issue, but upon probable cause, supported by oath or affirmation, and particularly describing the place to be searched, and the person or things to be seized.

Provisions similar to this are found in the constitutions of every state. But even if the states did not have such provisions, state searches and seizures were limited in 1952 as a result of federal judicial review. The Fourteenth Amendment to the federal Constitution, adopted in 1868 as one of the Civil War Amendments, provides that no state shall deprive any person "of life, liberty, or property, without due process of law." Ever since the 1920's, the Supreme Court has held that "due process" includes those rights in the first eight amendments to the federal Constitution that are basic to our system of "ordered liberty" in America, such as freedom of speech, press, religion, and assembly. In 1949, in a case called *Wolf* v. *Colorado,** the Supreme Court held that the Fourth Amendment's guaran-

---

* Official citations for all cases mentioned will be found in the Table of Cases at the end of this section.

tee against unreasonable searches and seizures was also part of the "due-process" clause of the Fourteenth Amendment, and therefore binding upon state officials. Violations by state officers thus became violations of the federal Constitution.

Before considering what practical effect this 1949 ruling had on the evidence obtained by state police in violation of the Fourth Amendment, we must turn specifically to telephone-tapping and microphoning.

In 1928, a 5-to-4 decision of the Supreme Court in *Olmstead* v. *United States* had held that wiretapping itself did not violate the Fourth Amendment. According to Chief Justice William H. Taft for the majority, telephone-users projected their voices outside the home; in addition, there was no seizure of anything tangible and no actual physical invasion of a person's premises. (Justices Oliver Wendell Holmes, Jr., and Louis D. Brandeis each contributed famous dissents challenging wiretapping as a "dirty business," a fundamental invasion of the citizen's constitutional privacy, and an inherently unreasonable method of police search.) The California constitutional provision on searches and seizures had received a similar construction by its courts, so that wiretapping violated neither the federal nor the California constitution.

As for the question of microphoning room conversations, the Supreme Court ruled in 1942 (*Goldman* v. *United States*) that federal officers who placed a sensitive microphone device on the wall of a room adjoining that of a suspect and heard his conversations, including those into the telephone receiver, had not violated the Fourth Amendment. The Court did not consider the question of whether the police had entered the suspect's room without a warrant to test or perfect their listening device; if an illegal entry had been made, this would violate the Fourth Amendment.

Although telephone-tapping and microphoning had not been construed as violating federal or state constitutions, there was legislation regulating these activities. In 1938, the Supreme Court decided that Section 605 of the Federal Communications Act, which said "No person not being authorized by the sender shall intercept and divulge or publish the meaning of such intercepted communication to any person . . . ," forbade federal officers to intercept telephone calls. Evidence so obtained was banned in federal trials. This was the "first *Nardone* case." In 1939, the Court held in the "second *Nardone* case" that evidence obtained by leads from wiretaps was also inadmissible, since it was in effect the "fruit of the poisonous tree." These rulings all dealt with federal tapping and federal trials. As far as state matters were concerned, a 1952 ruling of the Supreme Court, *Schwartz* v. *Texas,* seemed to hold that telephone-tapping by state police did violate the Federal Communications Act; however, the Court held that the state courts were free to decide whether such "illegal" wiretap evidence could be received in state trials.

This leads to the question of admissibility of evidence. Even when the conduct of federal or state police in securing evidence has been illegal, the question of whether the evidence—even if reliable, competent, and relevant —should be admitted in trials is a different issue from whether the means used to obtain it are legal. A 1914 decision of the Supreme Court, *Weeks* v. *United States,* established that illegally obtained evidence may *not* be used in federal trials. The federal "exclusionary rule" is based on the policy of deterring police misconduct by preventing the government from profiting from illegality; the risk of some guilty persons going free because of such a ban is considered less important than frustrating official lawlessness. The states, in considering this same question for their own courts, produced divided responses through the 1950's. A majority of the states (thirty-one) rejected the federal rule and admitted illegal evidence in state courts, feeling that the proper remedy for police misconduct was prosecution or disciplining of the offending officers, rather than freeing guilty persons because "the constable blundered." The remaining states followed the federal rule. In its 1949 ruling in the *Wolf* case, applying the Fourth Amendment to the states, the Supreme Court had held that the states were free to accept or reject the exclusionary doctrine for themselves.

Finally, there were state laws in 1952 covering both microphoning and telephone-tapping. Several states, such as California and Massachusetts, authorized police use of "bugging" devices. Thirty-eight states had laws forbidding wiretapping, but these were almost completely ineffectual. Only one state, New York, supervised police wiretapping by court warrants. Several states, such as Louisiana, gave police the right to tap wires on their own authority. In the thirty-eight states outlawing the interception of telephone or telegraph messages, none specified that this applied to the police, and as of 1952 no state Supreme Court had interpreted these laws as forbidding police wiretapping.

To summarize the law, therefore, when Russell Mason began to describe his "bugging" operation, the situation was as follows:

1. Illegal entries into a person's home—without proper warrants issued by a court—violated the federal Constitution when done by federal officials, state Constitutions when done by state officials, and the "due-process" clause of the Fourteenth Amendment to the federal Constitution when done by state officials. Evidence obtained by illegal entry was inadmissible in federal courts, but each state could decide for itself whether or not it wished to admit such evidence in its court trials.

2. Telephone-tapping did not violate the federal or state constitutions. It did violate a federal statute, and some state statutes. Wiretap evidence was not admissible in federal trials. It was admissible in the courts of thirty-one states, regardless of the state's wiretap law. In the other seventeen states, it would be inadmissible if the state forbade wiretapping, but no such cases had ever been so decided in state courts on police wiretapping.

3. Microphoning or electronic eavesdropping did not violate the federal or state constitutions. There was no federal legislation on this matter, no state law forbade it for police officials, and a few states specifically authorized police to employ electronic eavesdropping in criminal investigations.

California: The Police Wiretapper's Friend

In 1861 California became the first state in the nation to pass legislation on wiretapping, with a law forbidding interception of telegraph messages. In 1905, a scandal in which a newspaper reporter bribed telephone-operators to let him listen to calls going to a rival paper led California to extend the antitap law to telephone communications. Although this provision, listed as Section 640 of the Penal Code, bars "every person" from tapping, only private wiretappers had been successfully prosecuted down to 1952. Neither police officials nor technicians employed by them were even indicted under Section 640, much less convicted, in those forty-seven years.

As for electronic eavesdropping, California passed a statute on this subject in 1941, again in response to sensational disclosures of eavesdropping in political cases. Section 653h of this Penal Code provides:

> Any person who, without consent of the owner, lessee, or occupant, installs or attempts to install or use a dictograph in any house, room, apartment, tenement, office, shop, warehouse, store, mill, barn, stable, or other building, tent, vessel, railroad car, vehicle, mine or any underground portion thereof, is guilty of a misdemeanor.

But as a result of powerful pressure from law-enforcement officials acting through the California Peace Officers Association, Section 653h went on to say:

> provided, that nothing herein shall prevent the use and installation of dictographs by a regular salaried peace officer expressly authorized thereto by the head of his office or department or by a district attorney, when such use and installation are necessary in the performance of their duties in detecting crime and in the apprehension of criminals.

At the time of the Irvine investigation, then, California had a broad statute forbidding "every person" to tap telephone lines, without specific exception for the police. However, the law had never been used to prosecute the steadily wiretapping California police departments in the 1930's and 1940's. As for eavesdropping, California law specifically permitted the use of "dictographs" by police on the authorization of superior officers, and officers were busily "bugging" throughout the state. The California constitution does contain a provision on searches and seizures similar to the Fourth Amendment to the federal Constitution. Like its federal counterpart and like California antiwiretap statutes, however, by 1952 this provision had not yet been interpreted as forbidding wiretapping or eavesdropping by state police.

Moreover, according to *People* v. *Mayen* in 1922, even illegally obtained evidence that was inadmissible in federal courts and that violated the California constitution or California statutes was admissible in the state's courts. If the police had committed some crime in obtaining the evidence, they could be prosecuted for improper conduct separately.

More on Russell Mason, the Law-Enforcer's Friend

That was the law in California and in the nation on December 3, 1952, when Russell Mason connected his microphone to a ceiling fixture in the hall of Patrick Irvine's home and ran the wires to a listening post in a nearby garage. As Cochran continued his examination of Mason, further details of the eavesdropping operation were unfolded:

> MR. COCHRAN: After [the installation] had been done did you receive some complaints from the officers in respect to the audio features of this reception?
> MR. MASON: Yes, sir, I did.
> MR. COCHRAN: What was that date?
> MR. MASON: That was around the 8th, December 8th.
> MR. COCHRAN: . . . And did you move the microphone on that date?
> MR. MASON: Yes, sir, I moved it from the original place over the light fixture in the hall to over the light fixture in the bedroom.

The reason for this reentry, Mason explained further, was the complaint from officers at the listening post that there was "a hum" on the line which prevented "a good clear recording." Moving the microphone on December 8, however, did not solve this problem. The officers continued to complain of humming sounds. So Mason went back to Irvine's house a third time and placed the "bug" over a hole inside the bedroom closet door.

During each of these visits to move the microphone, Mason testified, he had the police officers go into Irvine's living room and bedroom and talk aloud so that reception could be tested and adjustments made. Mason's direct examination concluded with his account of removing the microphone on January 5, 1952, during the arrest. With Irvine, Inspector Kennedy, several police officers, and three newspaper photographers watching him, he climbed down from the attic holding the wires and the disconnected microphone.

Mason was cross-examined extensively by Defense Attorney McConnell, who led him through a series of questions about the fidelity of room recordings, the various entries to Irvine's home, and the exact manner in which the microphone was placed and moved. McConnell brought out the fact that the microphone would and did pick up conversation into the telephone, and if the party calling Irvine were talking loudly enough, both sides of the conversation might be overheard.

Mason did not testify again in the *Irvine* case. However, his pre-1952 activities as a "recording engineer" were to figure prominently in the press during later stages of the Irvine appeal and its aftermath. Mason began doing microphone eavesdropping as a private investigator in 1928. He moved to Los Angeles in the late 1930's as a full time "recording engineer," and he was soon doing 25 per cent of his work for private clients and 75 per cent for police agencies. His eavesdropping assignments included work for police departments in San Francisco, Oakland, Long Beach, Los Angeles, San Diego, and other cities. He also worked for the district attorney in Los Angeles and other counties, as well as for such public agencies as the State Medical Board, the State Narcotics Bureau, and the state attorney general's office. Between 1940 and 1956, Mason estimated that he had installed over 500 "bugs" in California for law-enforcement officers—in offices, stores, homes, hotel rooms, and automobiles. Between 1940 and 1950, he was employed as the "official eavesdropper" for the Los Angeles district attorney's office, with as many as seven microphone installations a week in operation.

In 1947, Mason's activities became a bit too public for his own good. An eavesdropping system he had installed in the State Building in Los Angeles was accidentally discovered. Mason had been hired by a special agent in the attorney general's office who wanted to check into the conversations of some state officials. In the course of installing his microphones, Mason had made some connections to the telephone switchboard and this activity provided the basis for his indictment—not under Section 640 for wire-tapping, but rather under a malicious-mischief law, for making unauthorized repairs on telephone equipment. He was given a ninety-day suspended jail sentence and placed on probation for one year. His law-enforcement clients probably accounted for this light sentence. Rumors that Mason's operation had provided him with "bulging files" on state officials must have worried some of California's public servants because a mysterious fire broke out in the middle of the affair, completely destroying his laboratory and filing cabinets.

Microphones and Stomach Pumps: When Is Process Due?

Meanwhile, the fruits of Russell Mason's work at 3916 East Second Street were ready to be presented to Judge Pierson and the jury. The People's second witness was Officer Jack Calori of the Long Beach police department's bookmaking detail. He described his actions in November and December when he had followed defendants Lippe and Curti as they drove to Irvine's house from the South Chestnut Street house and from the Red Onion Café; he was then asked by Cochran to relate the conversations of

Lippe and Irvine that he had heard while at the listening post on December 4. McConnell was on his feet at once, stating that any evidence obtained by microphone

> was a violation of the constitutional rights of the defendant Irvine as set forth in the Fourth Amendment to the Constitution of the United States. . . . This same exact provision is found in the Constitution of California as Section 19. . . . [In support of this contention], I wish to call your Honor's attention to a case [that] possibly you know, the federal case of *People* v. *Rochin*, and later termed the case of *Rochin* v. *the State of California.*

The *Rochin* case had been decided by the United States Supreme Court on January 2, 1952, and had been well publicized in California newspapers. Its facts had been summarized by Justice Felix Frankfurter in his opinion for the Court:

> Having "some information that [the petitioner here] was selling narcotics," three deputy sheriffs of the County of Los Angeles, on the morning of July 1, 1949, made for the two-story dwelling house in which Rochin lived with his mother, common-law wife, brothers and sisters. Finding the outside door open, they entered and then forced open the door to Rochin's room on the second floor. Inside they found petitioner sitting partly dressed on the side of the bed, upon which his wife was lying. On a "night stand" beside the bed the deputies spied two capsules. When asked, "Whose stuff is this?" Rochin seized the capsules and put them in his mouth. A struggle ensued, in the course of which the three officers "jumped upon him" and attempted to extract the capsules. The force they applied proved unavailing against Rochin's resistance.

Rochin had then been handcuffed and taken to a hospital. He had been strapped to a table and his mouth had been forced open.

> At the direction of one of the officers a doctor forced an emetic solution through a tube into Rochin's stomach against his will. This "stomach pumping" produced vomiting. In the vomited matter were found two capsules which proved to contain morphine.

Charged with possession of morphine, Rochin had been tried, convicted, and sentenced to sixty days in prison. "The chief evidence against him was the two capsules," Justice Frankfurter had noted. Rochin had appealed his conviction to the California District Court of Appeal. Even though that Court had held that the police officers "were guilty of unlawfully breaking into and entering defendant's room and were guilty of unlawfully assaulting and battering defendant while in the room," and even though they were also "guilty of unlawfully assaulting, battering, torturing and falsely imprisoning the defendant at the alleged hospital," the District Court had affirmed the conviction because of the California rule allowing illegally obtained evidence in court. On this basis, the California Supreme Court had denied Rochin's petition for a hearing.

But the United States Supreme Court had unanimously reversed Rochin's conviction, with eight Justices participating (Justice Minton did not take part). Justice Frankfurter, joined by five of his colleagues, had held that the illegal "search and seizure" of Rochin's person had constituted a denial of "due process of law" guaranteed against state infringement by the Fourteenth Amendment, according to the 1949 *Wolf* precedent. The existing Supreme Court test of whether due process had been violated, Frankfurter had said (quoting from earlier opinions by Justice Benjamin N. Cardozo), was whether the state had deprived a person of rights "implicit in the concept of ordered liberty" and "so rooted in the traditions and conscience of our people as to be ranked as fundamental." Frankfurter had gone on:

> The proceedings by which this conviction was obtained do more than offend some fastidious squeamishness or private sentimentalism about combatting crime too energetically. This is conduct that shocks the conscience. Illegally breaking into the privacy of the petitioner, the struggle to open his mouth and remove what was there, the forcible extraction of his stomach's contents—this course of proceeding by agents of government . . . [constitutes] methods too close to the rack and the screw to permit of constitutional differentiation.

In fact, the Court had held that these police violations were so shocking as to demand that the other part of the *Wolf* precedent (to allow state courts to admit illegal evidence if they wished) be set aside for the case at hand; the capsules of morphine were not allowed to be used in evidence against Rochin. In refusing to allow the evidence to be used, Justice Frankfurter had commented tartly: "To sanction the brutal conduct [by allowing the evidence] . . . would be to afford brutality the cloak of law. Nothing would be more calculated to discredit law and therefore to brutalize the temper of a society." Justices Black and Douglas had voted to reverse the conviction on the ground that Rochin had been deprived of his privilege against self-incrimination in the Fifth Amendment to the federal Constitution, which provides that "No person . . . shall be compelled in any criminal case to be a witness against himself. . . ." This Amendment, Black and Douglas said, was a limit upon the states as well, through the Fourteenth Amendment.

When McConnell raised the *Rochin* case in his objection to Officer

Calori's testimony about eavesdropped conversations, Judge Pierson called McConnell and Cochran into his chambers. This was done so that the legal discussion would not be heard by the jury and possibly influence their determination. In Judge Pierson's chambers, Cochran argued that "the Rochin case turns entirely on due process," and on the shocking physical character of stomach pumping, while the conduct in Irvine's case involved no such physical mistreatment. He added that the law in California ever since *People* v. *Mayen* in 1922, which had been followed "no less than 200 times" by California courts, was that evidence inadmissible in federal trials or obtained in violation of the California constitution was admissible in the state's courts if otherwise relevant and trustworthy.

Judge Pierson was persuaded by Cochran's argument and overruled McConnell's objection. He also overruled McConnell's contention that admission of the conversations would be a violation of Section 640 forbidding telephone-tapping, since this case dealt merely with "bugging." When the judge, counsel, and stenographer returned to the courtroom, the examination of Calori resumed. He gave a very brief description of conversations overheard on December 4 and 17 and, after desultory cross-examination, left the stand.

"Babe Gave Me Three Horses in That Race. . . ."

The next witness, Officer Charles Gautt, provided extensive testimony about conversations in the Irvine house, beginning with talks on December 17, 1951. Judge Pierson instructed him not to summarize the conversations but to relate them in dialogue from his notes. Gautt did so:

> One voice said "Joe wanted 40 and I figured I would hold him 60." The other voice said "Joe only wanted 10 dollars." And the same voice said something about paid 5.60. . . . The first voice said something about laying off money you haven't got and "When you lay it off my book, that's two separate books, just as separate as if you was giving it to Joe Irvine or somebody else as far as my book is concerned."
>
> The second party said, "Then I made a mistake. I had 45-across on the board. We made it 6-across. Bob only wanted 15-across. Bruce had enough on that horse."
>
> The first party said something about "It goes on his sheet or don't give it to him." The second party said, "Babe gave me three horses in that race. She come in with 5-and-5."

Gautt provided five typewritten pages of testimony from the conversation of December 17. Although reels of tape were later introduced as an exhibit in the trial, along with transcripts paralleling the portions the officers were reciting from their notes, the tapes themselves were never played to the jury.

Officer Gautt also gave testimony describing how the fluorescent powder "plant" was arranged. When enough incriminating conversation had been assembled, the police were ready to make their arrest; they wanted to do so in such a way as to seize physical evidence and establish proof of the relationship between bookmaking at South Chestnut Street and Irvine's home. On several occasions, Curti and a woman had been observed driving from the South Chestnut Street house to Irvine's, carrying bundles the officers believed to be bookmaking records. At 5:35 P.M. on January 5, Gautt related, Curti and the woman (Audie Greer) left the South Chestnut Street house by car. Gautt followed, dressed in plain clothes and in an unmarked car. At a prearranged point, he moved ahead of the Curti car. Then two motorcycle officers and a patrol car containing Officers Jacobsen and Dulaney stopped both Gautt's and Curti's cars. Everyone was told to get out and stand with his hands up. The officers explained that a liquor store had been held up and all new dark-colored Fords were being stopped because that was the type of vehicle used by the bandit. A gun was "found" in Gautt's belt and he was ostentatiously taken to the patrol car. Curti's person and car were searched, and Audie Greer's bundle of papers were examined. This examination was done by Officer Jacobsen, whose hands had been dusted with an invisible white crystalline powder, which was now on the bundle of papers being carried to Irvine's home.

The police gave Curti time to get to Irvine's and soon heard him (over the microphone) telling Irvine about being stopped at a roadblack for some liquor bandit. At 7:00 P.M., immediately after Curti and Audie Greer left the house, the officers entered and arrested Irvine. An immediate examination of Irvine's hands under ultraviolet rays disclosed fluorescent powder on them and on the betting papers in the drawer of the desk in Irvine's bedroom.

The next police witness, Officer Leonard Hermansen, provided page after page of dialogue overheard between December 3 and January 5. Many of these snatches of talk, unlike those recited by Officers Calori and Gautt, were conversations into the telephone:

> I heard the sound of a 'phone being dialed. I heard Mr. Irvine's voice. . . . I heard Mr. Irvine say, "Can I speak to Jamoke?" Then I heard Mr. Irvine say, "In the first place you've got the horse down wrong." Then I heard him say, "In the 8th, 2 to win." Then I heard him say "King's Boy, 2 to win. In the fourth, Handy Display. In the fifth, Limbo Junior, 2 to win. I've got some more for you. In the third, Clam Digger. . . ."

Mrs. Irvine was a working helpmate to her husband, and her telephone conversations were also recorded and testified to by Officer Hermansen. For example:

I heard the 'phone ring and I heard Mrs. Irvine's voice. I heard her say, "Wait a minute. I was down getting my laundry." Then I heard her say a lot of "Um-hums." Then I heard her say, "I'll write them down and mark them across the board. F-9. F-34. T-910."

We Had a Little Key . . . and No Warrant

After Officer Hermansen had spent a day reciting his notes, McConnell cross-examined him. Irvine's counsel particularly wanted to know how the police and Mason had entered Irvine's house to install and then move their listening equipment. Hermansen replied that he had simply "unlocked the door and walked in."

MR. McCONNELL: Did you have a key?
MR. HERMANSEN: I did.
MR. McCONNELL: Did Irvine give it to you?
MR. HERMANSEN: No.
MR. McCONNELL: A pass key?
MR. HERMANSEN: No, it was a regular house key.

McConnell was to return to this point later.

After Officer Donald Dulaney had testified about the roadblock affair and the arrest of Curti, Officer Lewis Jacobsen was called. He was an expert on bookmaking language and operations, having had six years on the bookmaking detail and a special course on "vice-control administration" at the University of Southern California, taught by a Los Angeles police department expert. Jacobsen explained fully that the ledgers, markers, betting sheets, and other materials found in Irvine's home and the conversations testified to were standard bookmaking materials and procedures.

During cross-examination, McConnell again raised the issue of the police entries. Jacobsen replied that the officers had a key.

MR. McCONNELL: I show you a key here and ask you, Is that the key that you used, if you would know?
MR. JACOBSEN: Yes, that is the key.
MR. McCONNELL: Where did you get it?
MR. JACOBSEN: I got it from a man that makes keys for a livelihood.

McConnell led Jacobsen to explain that on "the first or second of December," the locksmith was brought to the Irvine house while the Irvines were out. "He had an apparatus . . . that . . . you push into the lock to locate the tumblers and then file the key until it [opens] the lock."

After Audie Greer (now a State's witness), Officer Frederick Good, and Detective William Stovall had added details on the surveillance and arrest of the Irvine defendants, Inspector Everett Kennedy took the witness stand. He described the events of the arrest of January 5, 1952, including the fact that he "told Irvine that we had planted a microphone in his house and that we had listened to conversations for over a month." McConnell then pressed hard at the basis for the arrest and its circumstances:

> MR. McCONNELL: Did you enter with the use of this key that I have just shown you or did you just knock at the door and have it opened?
> MR. KENNEDY: Didn't knock at the door. Sgt. Jacobsen put that in the lock and opened the door.

McConnell then asked what Inspector Kennedy said to Irvine about searching the house:

> I told Mr. Irvine that we had made a legal arrest, that we had the right and we intended to search the entire house for evidence in our case, and that we were looking specifically for old records, and if he would tell us where they were it would keep us from searching the house.
> MR. McCONNELL: That statement of yours, that you had made a legal arrest, and that you had a right to search the place, that wasn't based on any search warrant you had in your possession, was it?
> MR. KENNEDY: I had no search warrant.

The final witness for the People was Officer Ralph Bradford, a handwriting expert, who testified that the betting records, the signatures on the federal wagering forms, and other physical evidence were all in the handwritings of Lippe, Curti, and Irvine.

It was now noon of Friday, April 11, 1952. Mr. Cochran announced, "The People rest."

When Silence Is Golden

On Monday, April 14, when the trial reconvened, McConnell announced:

> Ladies and gentlemen of the jury, your Honor, Mr. Cochran. The defendants will not take the stand in this case and will rest their defense upon the presumption of innocence, their rights under the Constitution of the United States and this state, and upon the factual weakness of the People's case on all counts, particularly on that in regard to conspiracy.

Normally, at this point in the trial the defense attorney would have "made his case." The defendants would have been called and examined about the charges, their characters and accomplishments unfolded to the jury, and witnesses produced to support the defense version of the central events and motivations.

Why McConnell chose not to put Irvine, Lippe, Curti, and Mrs. Irvine on the stand is not difficult to imagine. Effective denial of the State's facts about the bookmaking activities was impossible. Furthermore, putting

Irvine on the stand to bring out his good character would have entitled the prosecution to cross-examine the defendant on his past activities. A brief look at Irvine's biography, as he wrote it in a long letter in 1954 to the court authorities, indicates why McConnell probably wanted to avoid that.

Irvine's letter described his early life in Wyatt, Louisiana, a hip injury that made manual labor difficult for him, and his early wanderings about the country in the 1920's and early 1930's. Then, it went on to narrate:

> So I came back to Long Beach, California, early in 1938, and was given an opportunity to make a living in bookmaking in a small way. During 1938 I married the lady who is now my wife, and in 1939 bought a lot and built the home in which I still reside. In 1940 I was arrested and convicted of bookmaking and served a year in jail, starting July, 1941. During this time my home was supported by my wife, who was employed by the Associated Telephone Co. Upon my release from jail in May, 1942, I was employed by the California Shipbuilding Co. at Long Beach, California, and worked there until the end of 1944, when my physical handicap again forced me to discontinue manual labor. During this period I bought a restaurant in the 100 block, on American Avenue, Long Beach, which I have operated at various locations in that block ever since. In 1948, I again started bookmaking, in a small way, and continued until my arrest for bookmaking in 1952.

The police record on Irvine, which was carefully nestled in Cochran's briefcase in the event that Irvine took the stand, would have added some further painful details for the defense to overcome. Irvine was first arrested in Gainesville, Texas, in 1927. His California dossier started with a prohibition-act violation in Long Beach in 1930. Between 1931 and 1946, Irvine had been arrested seven times in Long Beach on charges including vagrancy, burglary, running a lottery, and drunkenness. Apart from paying fines and receiving suspended sentences, he had served a year in county jail for bookmaking in 1941.

Irvine's explanation of his conduct would ordinarily have been another major part of the defense case. In his 1954 letter, Irvine provides us with about what he would have said had he testified on this point. While admitting that what he did was a violation of law, he added:

> I consider it a minor offense, considering the fact that the State of California has declared itself in, to the extent of several million dollars a year, on funds realized from betting on horses. I mean the State's cut from legalized racing, and betting under the Pari-mutual [sic] System. . . . I fail to understand how the law can make it a crime to engage in horse race betting to the extent of a few thousand dollars, on one side of the fence, and declare it legal to bet a million a day on the other side. Another thing I feel is wrong, is the giving of a monopoly to the horse-racing fraternity, to the extent that it is illegal to make any kind of a bet

on any other kind of sport. There have been more men ruined and homes desolated and broken up by the Pari-mutual system, than there ever has been by hand-book makers. Most bets with bookmakers are very small. If a man bets a dollar with a bookmaker, even one every day, he would lose only seven dollars in a week. I know, in my own case, that I have refused bets from my clients when I knew that they were over-extending themselves.

Given the solid factual basis of the State's case, then, and the perils of testimony by the defendants, no witnesses were put on for Irvine and his colleagues.

The defense having rested, Cochran made the first closing statement. He laid out for the jury each of the elements of proof of bookmaking in violation of Section 337a, and he maintained that the testimony in the trial had "clearly established" that these charges were valid. McConnell's closing statement was part law and part an appeal to the jury's discretion. He challenged the legality of the police intrusions into Irvine's privacy and called on the jury to consider this in their deliberations. He also pointed to the widespread betting done off-track by many thousands of persons and said that these defendants had not done anything terribly wrong, even if it was forbidden by statute.

Enter the "Twelve Good Men and True"

After a short rebuttal from Cochran, Judge Pierson read a series of instructions to the jury to guide them in their deliberations. Such instructions are often based upon drafts submitted by the government and the defense, with the judge accepting those he feels correct or formulating his own versions. Over McConnell's objections, Judge Pierson accepted two key instructions from the People and read them to the jurors. The first advised the jurors to ignore "any trespass which you may find to have been committed." The defendants might sue the police later on for trespassing said the Judge, but that, "has no part in this trial." The other disputed instruction told the jurors to consider all evidence introduced "irrespective of the manner by which such evidence has been obtained . . . ," specifically, the evidence obtained by the planted microphone. Such evidence, Judge Pierson said, "is legally admissible in this State the same as any other competent evidence."

The next day, April 15, the jury reached its verdict. The three defendants were found not guilty on the conspiracy charge of Count 1. Irvine and Curti were found guilty of the other four counts and Lippe was found guilty of Counts 2, 4, and 5. The three men were continued at liberty, on bail, and May 9 was set for a hearing on probation requests, on McConnell's motion for a new trial, and on sentencing (if a new trial were denied).

At the hearing on May 9, McConnell tried to convince Judge Pierson that a new trial was called for, especially because of the *Rochin* case. He acknowledged California's admission rule, "and I am not asking your Honor to be a crusader or to overrule those decisions of the higher court. . . ." But, he argued, here was an "aggravated breach of the defendant's constitutional rights," and the verdict should be put aside. Judge Pierson was still not persuaded. "No matter how I might feel about that type of evidence," the Judge responded, no physical violence was used and the *Rochin* case was not in point. "If the [California] Supreme Court, as you say . . . [sees] fit to change the law, let them do it in this case. The motion for a new trial will be denied."

On May 14, Judge Pierson announced his sentence. First, he commented:

> I do not make the laws that govern this country and I realize at times it is pretty difficult to . . . legislate people's morals. Yet . . . these laws are made and it is like playing a football game. We have rules by which we play and we have rules by which we live. Now, if anybody else . . . was going to take it into their own hands and determine what rules they would abide by and what rules they would not abide by, then organized society, as such, is just not going to function.

Judge Pierson added:

> What is Mr. Irvine's attitude? Mr. Irvine says in effect, "I don't give a darn. I am going to live this way, the way I want, and I am going to do this." Now I cannot subscribe to that. . . . I have never felt good after I sent a man to jail. It makes me upset . . . but Irvine cannot get by with deals like this and someone has to impress him and I am going to be the one that has to decide the matter.

Then Judge Pierson announced Irvine's sentence: on Count 2, one year in county jail; on Count 3, six months imprisonment, to be suspended if Irvine paid a fine of $1,500 in three installments within ninety days, plus three years probation; on Counts 4 and 5, six months imprisonment (suspended) on each and a three-year probation. Lippe and Curti were each sentenced to six months in prison (five of which were suspended), a $500 fine, and three-year probations. McConnell asked that Irvine be freed on $3,000 bond, since he had filed an appeal. This was done, and after Judge Pierson delivered a short lecture to Patrick Irvine, the trial in Superior Court was officially at an end.

Along the Appellate Avenue to the Supreme Court

After trial in the Superior Courts of California, if a defendant chooses to appeal, his next step is the District Court of Appeal. California has five District Courts located geographically throughout the state. In the Los

Angeles District Court, there are four divisions, each with three justices. Vacancies on the District Court of Appeals are filled by the governor. At the first state-wide election more than fifty days after appointment, the electorate votes on the new appointees by answering the ballot question, "For associate justice, District Court of Appeals, Second Appellate District, Division Three. Shall Jonathan J. Jones be elected to the office for the term expiring January 1968?" Election is for a twelve-year term.

Irvine, the only one of the three defendants to appeal his case, had his case heard in Division Two, District Court of Appeal for the Second Appellate District, before Presiding Justice Minor Moore and Associate Justices W. Turney Fox and Marshall F. McComb. In his written brief and oral argument, McConnell presented two points: the first centered on the violation of due process; the second dealt with the "improper" instructions given by Judge Pierson. Mrs. Elizabeth Miller, deputy attorney general of California and a seasoned appellate lawyer, submitted a brief for the People and made the oral argument. Once the *Irvine* case left the Superior Court level, she and other members of the attorney general's staff would be responsible for defending the conviction (and the means employed to obtain it) against attack from Irvine's counsel.

On October 2, 1952, the District Court unanimously affirmed Irvine's conviction, reciting the prevailing rule on admissibility of illegally obtained evidence and finding no error in the charges to the jury.

McConnell then took Irvine's case to the final judicial tribunal in California, the California Supreme Court, located in San Francisco. This body has a chief justice and six associate justices, selected in the same manner and for the same terms of office as district justices. The Supreme Court does not have to hear every case presented to it; rather, it has discretion to review those appeals which it considers important to consider. Only about one out of five requests for hearings is granted. On October 30, 1952, by a 5-to-2 vote and without issuing an opinion, the California Supreme Court refused to hear Irvine's petition. The two dissenters, Justices Carter and Schauer, were long-standing dissenters from the California admissibility doctrine. Irvine now faced the question of whether he should try to appeal his case to the United States Supreme Court.

So far, only minor reports of his arrest, trial, conviction, and appeal had been carried in the California press. More newsworthy people and more serious crimes in which "bugging" was being used had been occupying public attention. The complete wiring of gambler Mickey Cohen's new house by the Los Angeles police at the time of its construction and the planting of a microphone in a Kleenex box beside the bed of a woman suspected of involvement in San Francisco and Los Angeles gambling operations were examples of the leading incidents. At the time that Irvine was being tried, a case that received great publicity was the bugging, by Russell Mason, of the bedroom of James Tarantino, a gossip-sheet publisher who was prosecuted and convicted of blackmailing California celebrities. Another central development in this period, stemming from the Mickey Cohen microphoning installation, was a suit filed in 1951 by A. L. Wirin, counsel of the American Civil Liberties Union Chapter of Southern California; this suit sought to enjoin Los Angeles Police Chief William Parker from using public funds to install "illegal" dictographs and microphones. In 1950, Parker had issued Order No. 826, authorizing bugging as long as prior permission was obtained by the police officers and confidential reports of the results were filed.

In November 1952, Irvine and McConnell began to consider strategy for appealing to Washington. McConnell, who was not experienced in arguing appeals before the Supreme Court, contacted a Washington attorney to argue the petition for certiorari, which asks the Justices to review the case. Under the Court's rules before July 1, 1954, a petition for certiorari had to be accompanied by a printed copy of the record;* in Irvine's case, this meant the printing of the 995-page transcript of the proceeding in Superior Court. The Washington attorney estimated the cost of such a printing at $3,500. Printing the clerk's transcript and the brief in support of the petition, plus the attorney's fee for filing the petition for certiorari, would cost $5,000 more. If the petition were granted, there would be an additional fee for writing a full brief and making the oral argument. Irvine did not have $8,500-plus.

Enter Morris Lavine, Appealing

Faced with this situation, McConnell called a Los Angeles specialist in appellate work, Morris Lavine, and asked him to handle the case. Lavine, who had entered law practice in Los Angeles in 1918, had a reputation as a skillful defendant's lawyer in criminal and civil-liberties cases. When he was not arguing his own cases, he was often ghostwriting appellate briefs for other lawyers.

Having argued a number of cases in the Supreme Court, Lavine was able to tell McConnell that printing the record was not an absolute requirement. Under the rules then in force in the Supreme Court, the Justices could grant permission to file for a petition of certiorari and use the typewritten record of the lower-court reporter. This was done when the cost of printing the record was beyond a defendant's means and the requirement would prevent presentation of important federal questions; Lavine had obtained such leave in *Kawakita* v. *United States.* He offered to handle the appeal for $1,000. If the petition were granted, he would be paid an additional sum for his time and trip to Washington. Actually, Lavine was attracted strongly to Irvine's appeal. "The case fascinated me," he recalled; "imagine placing a microphone in a married man's bedroom, after entering

---

* Under the rules after July 1, 1954, a printed record is required only after a petition for certiorari is granted.

his house like an ordinary burglar with special keys . . . to catch a man making book!" Later he added, "It was the type of appeal I would rather handle than go to a show."

Lavine's motion to proceed on the typewritten record and his petition for certiorari (with accompanying brief in support of the petition) were filed in the Supreme Court on January 1953. The mathematical chances of having one's petition granted are strongly against a petitioner. At the term of Court during which Lavine filed, 665 petitions for certiorari were filed, but only 104 were granted. "The Supreme Court," Chief Justice Fred Vinson once noted, "is not, and never has been, primarily concerned with the correction of errors in lower court decisions."

> In almost all cases within the Court's appellate jurisdiction, the petitioner has already received one appellate review of his case. The debates in the Constitutional Convention make clear that the purpose of the establishment of one supreme national tribunal was, in the words of John Rutledge of South Carolina, "to secure the national rights & uniformity of Judgmts." The function of the Supreme Court is, therefore, to resolve conflicts of opinion on federal questions that have arisen among lower courts, to pass upon questions of wide import under the Constitution, laws, and treaties of the United States, and to exercise supervisory power over lower federal courts. If we took every case in which an interesting legal question is raised, or our *prima facie* impression is that the decision below is erroneous, we could not fulfill the Constitutional and statutory responsibilities placed upon the Court. To remain effective, the Supreme Court must continue to decide only those cases which present questions whose resolution will have immediate importance beyond the particular facts and parties involved.

Irvine proved to be fortunate in his relations with the Justices. Leave to proceed on the typewritten record was granted and the Court examined Irvine's petition for certiorari. Lavine argued that four fundamental questions should be passed on by the Justices. Two related to the federal wagering stamp and its use in Irvine's trial. The other two revolved around the eavesdropping, arguing that due process demanded rejection of such evidence and that the use here deprived Irvine of his right to a fair trial.

On March 9, 1953, the Supreme Court granted the petition for certiorari. Lavine began writing his brief, and attorneys for the People began writing theirs.

Keeping the Wolf from the Door
Perhaps the most serious block to Irvine's chances for success in the Supreme Court was the 1949 *Wolf* case. According to this precedent, as mentioned earlier, six Justices had held that while "the security of one's privacy against arbitrary intrusion by the police" is part of a person's right to due process under the Fourteenth Amendment, the states could allow such

illegally obtained evidence to be used in state trials. A Court majority felt that the choice between exclusion of evidence and civil or criminal prosecutions against the police should be up to the states to make. Since thirty-one states admitted illegally obtained evidence in 1949, this majority obviously did not consider exclusion to be essential to ordered liberty in a free society. If the *Wolf* precedent were held to control, Irvine's conviction was likely to be sustained. But if he could fit his case into the *Rochin* compartment as an invasion of privacy so shocking as to require exclusion of evidence, his conviction based on illegally obtained evidence was apt to be reversed.

When *Wolf* had been decided, the Supreme Court majority supporting the rule consisted of Chief Justice Fred Vinson and Associate Justices Felix Frankfurter, Stanley Reed, Robert Jackson, Harold Burton, and Hugo Black. The three dissenters had been Justices Frank Murphy, Wiley Rutledge, and William O. Douglas. When Irvine's case was argued before the Supreme Court on November 30, 1953, the Court's personnel had undergone several changes, none of which seemed especially heartening to Irvine's prospects. Two of the dissenters in *Wolf,* Murphy and Rutledge, had died in 1949 and had been replaced by Tom C. Clark and Sherman Minton, men who had established themselves quickly as conservatives in the area of civil liberties and criminal procedure. In place of Chief Justice Vinson sat Earl Warren of California, whose career as crusading district attorney of Alameda County, attorney general, and anticrime governor gave little indication that he would be generously disposed toward a clearly guilty bookmaker or that he would be strictly inclined toward the California police.

Actually, the area of search and seizure was so confused and fluid that rigid "bloc" analysis of the Justices was unwise. One could never quite tell how the Court would treat such cases. Justice Black, for example, a stout exponent of the "absolute" Bill of Rights and of maximum civil-liberties activism from the Court, seemed to view the Fourth Amendment as less absolute than other Amendments.* He had joined the majority in *Wolf* and in other search cases affirming convictions against claims of Fourth Amendment deprivations. Justice Frankfurter, on the other hand, generally described as an exponent of judicial self-restraint and permissive toward state action, had written the outraged opinion of the Court in the *Rochin* case and had dissented vigorously in the wiretapping decisions in *Goldman, On Lee,* and comparable cases. But to further compound the complexities, he had also written the opinion in the *Wolf* case.

---

* It should be noted that the Fourth Amendment's command is that searches and seizures not be "unreasonable," while the First Amendment states that "Congress shall make *no* law" abridging freedom of speech, press, assembly, and religion. This difference in standard has affected Justice Black's reaction to search-and-seizure cases.

Actually, the Supreme Court of 1954 would be considering electronic eavesdropping from a remarkably broad base of experience. Jackson and Clark had been attorneys general of the United States and had authorized FBI wiretapping. Both had refused to prosecute state officials for violation of Section 605 of the Federal Communications Act. Black, during his years as a United States Senator, had outraged conservatives by subpoenaing the original copies of telegraph messages from Western Union to show how utility companies were lobbying to defeat New Deal legislation. Shortly after graduation from law school, Frankfurter had served in the United States attorney's office for the southern district of New York under Henry Stimson and had formed the opinion there that wiretapping and eavesdropping were simply not essential to effective law enforcement. He had grown more convinced of this view as the years had passed. Warren, as already noted, had been a California prosecutor when wiretapping and eavesdropping were standard procedure for prosecutors. As California's governor, he had deplored political wiretapping but had not opposed police use of the technique.

The experience of these Justices was not precisely in point for the *Irvine* case, however, and it is generally risky to assume that men carry all of their pre-Court views into their opinions when they become Justices. All that this biographical data suggests is that the Court's members had informed ideas about this field and that discussion at the conference table was likely to be lively.

The briefs in the *Irvine* case arrived at the Supreme Court in the fall of 1953. Irvine's was filed on October 31, California's on November 23. Earlier, on March 9, 1953, the Supreme Court had narrowed some of the issues in the *Irvine* case by deciding in *United States* v. *Kahriger* that the federal wagering tax was constitutional. Six Justices had held that it did not intrude on the reserved powers of the states or violate the bookmaker's privilege against self-incrimination. The use of the stamp as evidence in a state prosecution had *not* been passed upon in the *Kahriger* case, and this remained as part of the debate in the briefs for Irvine and California.

Oral argument before the Supreme Court was scheduled for Monday, November 30. It is here that the Justices, through questions to counsel about the facts and the implications of the arguments being offered, begin to get the intimate "feel" for the case that is essential to wise judgment.

Before the Bar of Justice

Before Monday, Lavine took a train to Washington and spent the morning at the Library of the Supreme Court reading the original record of the *Wolf* case. When he opened his argument for Irvine before the Supreme Court on Monday morning, he recalled recently,

I barely had time to address the court when Justice Frankfurter shot this question at me:

"How do you distinguish this case on the facts from *Wolf* v. *Colorado?*"

I answered: "*Wolf* v. *Colorado* was an abortion case, where the officers after seizing records in the doctor's office went out to the patients whose names they secured. They didn't find the patients in the office and they didn't place a microphone in the doctor's office to listen to him. In the *Irvine* case, the officers made a key to the house, and like common burglars, went in and placed a microphone to learn if he was taking bets . . . and listened to this married couple for a month to get information about bookmaking."

Frankfurter then asked Lavine, "Do you think it was worse than taking records from a doctor's office to get the names of his patients?" "I do," Lavine replied. "It is as bad as sticking a stomach pump into a man to compel him to throw up the evidence, as in *Rochin*. . . . I can't think of any more shocking invasion of privacy than to stick a microphone into a man's bedroom secretly."

When the State's turn came, the oral argument was presented by Mrs. Miller, deputy attorney general, and Clarence Linn, assistant attorney general. Several of the Justices bore down heavily on counsel for the State, revealing their shock at the facts. Chief Justice Warren read Section 653h of the California Penal Code to Linn, and asked whether the consent of the chief of police or district attorney had been secured to place the microphone. Linn stated that he believed no such permission had been obtained. The Chief Justice remarked that such unauthorized use seemed to be a crime on the part of the police officers. Linn, who had argued the *Rochin* case in the Supreme Court, tried to veer the argument back to the *Wolf* principle and away from *Rochin*. However, the questioning concentrated heavily on the police conduct, with little discussion on the value of excluding illegally obtained evidence.

When the oral argument was concluded, several lawyers in the courtroom congratulated Lavine on having won his case, since the questions from Warren, Frankfurter, Jackson, and others seemed to indicate deep dissatisfaction with California's position. "Everyone thought the Chief was with me," Lavine noted, "but knowing his attitude toward bookmaking, I did not feel that way."

After hearing oral argument, the Supreme Court considers the case at the conference held at the end of the week. Full discussion is held among the Justices, and a vote is usually taken the same week that the case is argued. Then drafts of the opinion for the Court and any concurring or dissenting opinions are written by the individual Justices and circulated to other members of the Court for comment. The case is then "brought back" to conference and a final vote is taken. (Between the first conference vote and the final one, Justices can and often do change their position as they reflect on the issues or read the drafts.) The debate in the conference room on the Irvine case was unusually heated and what had seemed a rather tawdry little appeal when it first arrived at the Court now seemed to be developing into a hearty *cause célèbre*. (It is significant to note that no organization filed an *amicus curiae* ["friend of the court"] brief in support of Irvine's civil-liberties claims, although such intervention is common in such cases as this. Neither the Southern California Civil Liberties Union nor the American Civil Liberties Union entered the case, nor did any of the various bar associations or other groups that had an ideological interest in vindicating freedom from police eavesdropping on bedroom conversations.)

Five Justices Make a Court: The Jackson Opinion

The Supreme Court's ruling in the *Irvine* case was handed down on February 8, 1954. The Court had voted 5 to 4 to affirm the conviction. There were five opinions: one by Jackson for himself, Warren, Reed, and Minton; one by Clark concurring in the majority result; a dissent by Black for himself and Douglas; a dissent by Frankfurter for himself and Burton; and an additional separate dissent by Douglas.

Jackson's opinion for the Court began by disposing of the claims for reversal based on the federal wagering act. Without discussing the question of self-incrimination, Jackson said that the act had been held constitutional in the *Kahriger* case, the information it required was intended to be made public, and the act specifically stated that no one should be exempt from prosecution by state law for engaging in such taxed activity.

"But the questions raised by the officers' conduct while investigating this case are serious," Jackson continued. These were clear violations of the citizen's constitutional right to privacy:

> Each of these repeated entries of petitioner's home without a search warrant or other process was a trespass, and probably a burglary, for which any unofficial person should be, and probably would be, severely punished. Science has perfected amplifying and recording devices to become frightening instruments of surveillance and invasion of privacy, whether by the policeman, the blackmailer, or the busybody. That officers of the law would break and enter a home, secrete such a device, even in a bedroom, and listen to the conversation of the occupants for over a month would be almost incredible if it were not admitted. Few police measures have come to our attention that more flagrantly, deliberately, and persistently violated the fundamental principle declared by the Fourth Amendment.

Jackson reviewed the *Wolf* case's unwillingness to apply the exclusionary-evidence rule to the states and said, "That holding would seem to control here." He dismissed the similarity of *Irvine* to *Rochin*. as the latter case had rested upon an element totally lacking here—coercion . . . applied by a physical assault upon his person to compel submission to the use of a stomach pump. This was the feature which led to a result in Rochin contrary to that in Wolf. . . . However obnoxious are the facts in the case before us, they do not involve coercion, violence or brutality to the person, but rather a trespass to property, plus eavesdropping.

To reverse Irvine's conviction, even though it was not within the *Rochin* rule, because it was "more shocking, more offensive" than the situation in *Wolf,* said Jackson, would leave the Court's rule of due process in search-and-seizure cases "so indefinite that no state court could know what it should rule in order to keep its processes on solid constitutional ground."

In support of this position, Jackson explained that until 1949 the Fourth Amendment's guarantees against searches and seizures had never been held to be part of the Fourteenth's guarantees of due process (and therefore binding on the states). As yet the states had not had sufficient time to re-evaluate their own policies of admission of illegally obtained evidence in state courts; he suggested tactfully that states "may wish further to reconsider" their evidentiary principle in light of *Wolf.*

But to upset state convictions even before the states have had adequate opportunity to adopt or reject the rule would be an unwarranted use of federal power. The chief burden of administering criminal justice rests upon state courts. To impose upon them the hazards of federal reversal for noncompliance with standards as to which this Court and its members have been so inconstant and inconsistent would not be justified. We adhere to Wolf as stating the law of search-and-seizure cases and decline to introduce vague and subjective distinctions.

Jackson's opinion concluded with the comment that there is "no lack of remedy if an unconstitutional wrong has been done in this instance without upsetting a justifiable conviction of this commonplace gambler." The Federal Civil Rights Act (passed during Reconstruction) makes it a crime for any person under color of law willfully to deprive anyone of his rights and privileges secured by the federal Constitution. Carefully indicating that he was speaking only for himself and Chief Justice Warren in this suggestion (and not for Justices Reed and Minton who joined the rest of this opinion), Jackson said: "We believe the Clerk of this Court should be directed to forward a copy of the record in this case, together with a copy of this opinion, for attention of the Attorney General of the United States."

(When Jackson delivered this opinion orally in the Courtroom, he commented extemporaneously that he and the Chief Justice would have to pay the postage for this forwarding since the Court disapproved of the action.)

Clark's Reluctant Consent

Justice Clark wrote a short concurring opinion joining in the result but not in all the reasoning of the Court's opinion. If he had been on the Court when the *Wolf* case had been decided, he said, he would have voted to apply the exclusionary rule in search-and-seizure cases to the states. Since the Court refused to overturn that precedent, he would vote "reluctantly" to stick to its letter rather than "sterilize" the rule by a "case-to-case approach" that would make for "uncertainty and unpredictability." He added, "Perhaps strict adherence to the tenor of [the *Wolf*] decision may produce needed converts for its extinction."

Black and Douglas Take the Fifth

Justice Black, joined by Justice Douglas, maintained that the Court should have reversed Irvine's conviction because it was based on evidence from the federal wagering act "extorted from him by the Federal Government in violation of the Fifth Amendment." Black and Douglas, who had dissented in the *Kahriger* case, said that even though that act had been held constitutional, the use of confessions forced under it to convict defendants in state courts should have been held unconstitutional. "I believe this frustrates a basic purpose of the Fifth Amendment—to free Americans from fear that federal power could be used to compel them to confess conduct or beliefs in order to take away their life, liberty or property."

Black added one last paragraph, objecting strongly to the call for action by the Attorney General as suggested by Jackson and Warren. That is "inconsistent with my own view of the judicial function in our government. Prosecution, or anything approaching it, should, I think, be left to government officers whose duty it is."

The Anti-Mechanics of Frankfurter and Burton

Justice Frankfurter, joined by Burton, dissented from what he regarded as the "mechanical" applications of the due-process clause and the *Wolf-Rochin* precedents. Judicial construction of due process called for flexibility, a "gradual process of judicial inclusion and exclusion," as the Court had said in the nineteenth century. Even though physical violence was absent in Irvine's case, "we have here . . . a more powerful and offensive control over the Irvines' life than a single, limited physical trespass." It would be highly unwise to "announce a new absolute, namely, that even the most reprehensible means for securing a conviction will not taint a verdict so long as the body of the accused was not touched by State officials."

Frankfurter replied in detail to Jackson's argument questioning the efficacy of the exclusionary rule. He concluded that to suggest other means to punish the illegal actions of the Long Beach police was to shirk the Court's duty. A new trial was demanded.

Douglas Takes the Fourth as Well

The final opinion, by Justice Douglas, related fully the "revolting" conduct of the police. Such "unconstitutional evidence" could not be used in state trials, Douglas said:

> It is no answer that the man is doubtless guilty. The Bill of Rights was designed to protect every accused against practices of the police which history showed were oppressive to liberty. The guarantee against unreasonable searches and seizures contained in the Fourth Amendment was one of those safeguards.

Deploring the *Wolf* case's original departure from principle, Douglas challenged the idea of a remedy through prosecution by the Attorney General. He described the overburdened status of the civil-rights section of the Department of Justice and the "hostile" greeting that Federal Civil Rights Act prosecutions of police officers had received from the Supreme Court in the past. He also added an appendix to his opinion showing how few prosecutions had been brought under that act.

> As long as courts receive the evidence, the police will act lawlessly and the rights of the individual will suffer. We should throw our weight on the side of the citizen and against lawless police. We should be alert to see that no *unconstitutional* evidence is used to convict any person in America.

The Aftermath of Irvine's Trials

After a petition for rehearing submitted by Lavine was quickly denied by the Supreme Court, Irvine's appeal was finished. No higher court was available. But while this specific case was over, the impact of the *Irvine* ruling was only beginning.

The *Irvine* case, unlike "big" Supreme Court decisions, drew little immediate attention from the national press. Most leading newspapers ignored *Irvine* completely. A few had minor news accounts. Only a handful wrote editorials. The St. Louis *Post-Dispatch,* on February 9, 1954, wrote the strongest editorial comment, denouncing it as "a judicial outrage" and a "terribly wrong decision."

> There are a shocking number of things wrong with this 5-to-4 decision, but undoubtedly the most distressing aspect of it is the fact that Chief Justice Warren is on the side which shuts its eyes to justice under the Constitution. Indeed it is by the vote of the new Chief Justice that the scales tip against the civil rights views of Justices Black, Douglas, Frankfurter and Burton and in favor of the strange position of Justices Reed, Jackson, Clark and Minton.

Justice Clark's "astonishing position" in following a rule he considered unwise was also criticized.

> Justice Clark is not obligated to follow any decision he does not believe in. Can it be that he is so little familiar with the history of the bench on which he sits that he does not know that Justices and the Court have reversed themselves many times when convinced of error?

Reviewing the facts and noting that what happened to "this miserable gambler can overtake any other citizen," the *Post-Dispatch* lamented that "once again the Supreme Court has joined in eroding the liberties of the American people. . . . A judgment so rank will not stand for long. The quicker it is expunged the better it will be!"

California Digests the Decision

Reaction in California law-enforcement circles was swift. In some ways, it resembled the stunned sensation of a man long used to kicking a mule who suddenly finds that the mule has kicked back, even lightly. The possibility of federal prosecution, while not terribly real, had at least been raised, and the California police became a bit edgy.

Reflecting this feeling, the district attorney of Los Angeles County, S. Ernest Roll, sent a letter on February 15, 1954, to the attorney general of California, Edmund Brown (now governor), asking for an official opinion on the meaning of the *Irvine* ruling for California law-enforcers. Specifically, Roll wanted to know whether a district attorney should refuse to prosecute new cases and move to dismiss existing cases based primarily on evidence such as in *Irvine* and whether police agencies had to "completely refrain" from such conduct hereafter. Roll also asked whether it would make any difference in either answer if the "bug" were installed in an office, hotel room, or place of business rather than a home.

Brown's answer was given on September 4, 1954. Briefly, his rulings were:

1. District attorneys could prosecute cases based on evidence such as that used in *Irvine* and they would not incur liability by doing so. This conclusion was based on the majority holdings of *Wolf, Irvine,* and the California cases rejecting the exclusionary-evidence rule. But, Brown went on to state, the district attorney's oath was to maintain and uphold the federal and California constitutions. That oath "commits him to a duty to defend and protect the rights of the people guaranteed thereunder . . . [and] conviction of the guilty by deprivation of constitutional rights imperils the freedom of the innocent." The district attorneys had therefore to review all such cases and decide whether it would be in the interests of the people of California to prosecute them.

2. Police officials who used such methods in private homes might be liable for both civil and criminal penalties. This applied to bugging in offices, hotel rooms, and places of business as well. This conclusion was put with a clarity that even a Los Angeles policeman could grasp:

> There can be no room for quibbling over the "holding" of the *Irvine* case. The articulate premise of the decision is that the officers involved violated Irvine's constitutional rights. Therefore, law enforcement officers who engage in such conduct violate their oath to support and follow the Constitution of the United States and the Constitution of the State of California.

To determine exactly what police conduct would be illegal, Brown reviewed the federal cases thoroughly. He concluded that the basic offense in the *Irvine* case was the trespass on Irvine's property, the unlawful entry. Listening without trespass had not been condemned. As for California's law allowing police to use dictographs, Brown brushed this statute aside swiftly, ruling that it could give no officer any right to violate the constitution of the nation or state, and police conduct "should be governed accordingly."

Many enforcement officials in California made hostile comments on the decision. Chief William Parker of Los Angeles and the city attorney saw the *Irvine* case as resting upon "a complete absence of facts on the question of the reasonableness of the quest under the circumstances." Clarence Linn commented later, "I believe that a man's home is his castle, but if he turns it into a bookmaking establishment, the reason for the rule ceases to exist."

How police officials would react in practice to the ruling of Attorney General Brown remained to be seen.

The Department of Justice Reads the Record

Another Attorney General had to be reckoned with—United States Attorney General Herbert Brownell. When the record of the *Irvine* case and the Supreme Court's opinion reached the Department of Justice, a full investigation was ordered, to be conducted by the Federal Bureau of Investigation. The FBI soon discovered that Russell Mason and the Long Beach police *had* been authorized to install a microphone in Irvine's house, contrary to what Assistant Attorney General Clarence Linn had thought and had informed Chief Justice Warren during oral argument. Assistant United States Attorney General Warren Olney III (himself a Californian and a Warren protégé) headed the Justice Department's criminal division. He stated officially that the eavesdropping had been done "under orders of the Chief of Police, who in turn was acting with the full knowledge of the District Attorney."

When an FBI agent interviewed Morris Lavine during the investigation, Lavine stated that Irvine would neither make a complaint nor aid in the prosecution of the officers. With his home and his restaurant in Long Beach, and given his criminal record, Irvine "would be harassed by the police for the rest of his life," Lavine said. Both Irvine and Lavine urged the Justice Department to drop the prosecution. While he and his counsel had invoked every possible guarantee of the state and federal constitutions during his trials, Irvine was too skilled a handicapper of realities (as well as of horses) to "take on the Los Angeles police force."

Looking over these facts, the Department of Justice concluded that it was "doubtful" whether a successful prosecution under the Federal Civil Rights Act could be maintained. It was decided that "it would be both useless and inadvisable to present [the] matter to the Federal grand jury." This decision, Olney has explained, "was largely influenced by the belief that the Government . . . would not be able to satisfy the rigid standard of intent [knowingly to deprive a person of his constitutional rights] imposed by the Supreme Court" in cases construing the Civil Rights Act. Particular mention was made of *Screws* v. *United States,* a Civil Rights Act case decided in 1945. There, the Supreme Court had reversed the conviction of a Georgia sheriff who had beaten a handcuffed Negro prisoner to death; a "specific intent" to deprive a person of rights expressly given by the Constitution or by court decisions interpreting the Constitution was required, the majority ruled, and this element had not been found in the Georgia trial. Those elements, Olney felt, would impair any possibility of proceeding against the Long Beach police. Consequently, the matter was closed.

The Nation Surveys Its Party Line

While the California community was digesting the *Irvine* case, a flood of wiretapping and eavesdropping incidents throughout the country focused public attention on the issue.

Eavesdropping news cropped up everywhere in the states. During February 1955, a central wiretap station in New York City was discovered; this listening post permitted its enterprising private-detective installers to monitor over 100,000 telephone lines in the plush mid-Manhattan area. Also in 1955, the district attorney of Philadelphia took it upon himself to release to the press the full transcripts of telephone taps he had ordered on the lines of out-of-town Teamsters Union organizers who the district attorney alleged were intending to raid a local union; no prosecutions were ever initiated against the wiretapped visitors. In 1954, an investment broker and a private detective in Chicago were caught tapping the line of a company the broker was thinking of purchasing. Also in Chicago in 1954, a local labor racketeer tapped the phones of the persons complaining about him to a federal grand jury. Taps by Maryland police in bookmaking cases in 1954–55 became so widespread that the Baltimore *Sun* attacked "wide-open, indiscriminate uses of wire tapping" in the state. In Las Vegas, Nevada, the public learned that hidden microphones were used by a newspaper editor to get proof of connections between state officials and prominent gamblers; in addition, it was revealed that many of the local brothels wired their rooms to collect "useful information" about important clients. In New Jersey, a state investigation in 1956 concluded that prosecutors and state troopers were tapping telephones despite the 1930 New Jersey statute forbidding such conduct. Private detectives were also doing a thriving business in the Garden State. These instances were paralleled by disclosures in Detroit, Kansas City, Portland (Oregon), and many other communities. Clearly, wiretapping and bugging were no longer—if they had ever been—a phenomenon restricted to the "eavesdropping capitals" of Washington, New York, and Los Angeles.

The years 1954 and 1955 also saw a series of dramatic and influential Congressional hearings into electronic eavesdropping. At one point, a private wiretapper even demonstrated to Congressmen at a committee hearing how he could sit in a legislator's outer office reading a magazine while secretly recording telephone calls made from the inner office. The display of parabolic microphones, transistor recorders, and "Buck Rogers" sound equipment, all in working order and not in blueprints, had a profound effect on the Congressional investigators, and their reaction was registered in the alarmed stories featured in the press. Proof that this public alarm represented more than just the usual concern of editors of liberal weeklies and civil libertarians was the fact that two major television networks raced one another in 1955 to see which could broadcast the first exposé of electronic eavesdroppers. Reverend Billy Graham's organization made a movie entitled *Wiretapper,* depicting the religious conversion of a man named Jim Vaus whose presalvation occupation had been that of a "professional earphones man" for both the police and gambler Mickey Cohen. The mass media steadily featured articles on wiretapping excesses in this period, and even Daddy Warbucks in the nationally syndicated comic strip "Little Orphan Annie" learned to his anger that agents of "the Syndicate" were tapping his calls.

Even more important than this concern itself was the fact that, for the first time since the 1920's, the states were beginning to take legislative steps to deal with wiretapping and the newer electronic-eavesdropping developments. The cold statistics of state action between 1954 and 1958 reveal something of a civil-liberties revolt by the legislatures. Eighteen states held legislative debates over tighter control laws in that four-year period. Three states—Maryland, Nevada, and Oregon—joined New York in putting police wiretapping under tight court-order controls, while writing clear and modernized prohibitions against wiretapping by private detectives. Two states, Pennsylvania and Illinois, banned all wiretapping completely, whether done by police agencies or by private persons, and excluded all wiretap evidence from their state courts. Five states went beyond telephone-tapping and enacted controls on all types of eavesdropping—by radio, microphone, or electric beam—on any form of conversation. Three states had judicial rulings that declared wiretapping to be illegal under existing state laws and excluded wiretap evidence from state trials. One state passed a law making Section 605 of the Federal Communications Act binding within the state in order to exclude all evidence obtained by wiretapping. Some municipalities passed ordinances to control wiretapping excesses. Baltimore, for example, enacted an ordinance in 1954 requiring the city police to obtain a court order before tapping telephones within the city limits.

Furthermore, these laws were not left to languish on the statute books. A deputy inspector and two plain-clothes men of the Brooklyn police force were dismissed for illegal wiretapping, and the two plain-clothes men pleaded guilty to criminal charges. Private tappers in New York, Chicago, and Portland (Oregon) were indicted and convicted. Included in this group was John Broady, probably the top New York wiretapper, who was sentenced to prison for two to four years and disbarred as an attorney. Even the federal government became active in enforcement of Section 605 against *private* violators. Between 1954 and 1961 there were twelve prosecutions brought involving twenty wiretappers. Ten of the cases resulted in convictions, and the wide distribution of cases—in Texas, Maryland, Louisiana, California, New York, North Carolina, Oregon, and Arkansas—made the new enforcement policy nationwide. The New York secretary of state withdrew licenses from private detectives who wiretapped or eavesdropped illegally, and this action cut private wiretapping facilities in that state even further.

California Changes Its Mind

In this new climate of public opinion on privacy, eavesdropping, and law enforcement, the State of California was not left untouched.

In 1955, the California Supreme Court found itself faced with the appeal of Charles H. Cahan and fifteen others, charged with conspiracy to engage in bookmaking in violation of Section 337a. An officer of the intelligence unit of the Los Angeles police, with Chief Parker's permission, had entered Cahan's house "through the side window of the first floor" and had supervised the installation of a mike under a chest of drawers. Lines were strung to a nearby garage where a listening post and recording station was established. It was almost a perfect duplication of the *Irvine* situation.

This time, the California Supreme Court did not brush the appeal aside. Instead, a 4-to-3 majority overruled *People* v. *Mayen* and its successors and placed California in the list of states that excluded illegally obtained evidence.

The presence of the United States Supreme Court's opinions in the *Irvine* case hung like fallout over the majority opinion. California Justice Roger Traynor noted the caustic censure by the Supreme Court of such methods of getting evidence, while noting that here the Los Angeles police blithely admitted to kicking doors in and forcing windows to gain entry.

> Thus, without fear of criminal punishment or other discipline, law enforcement officers, sworn to support the Constitution of the United States and the Constitution of California, frankly admit their deliberate, flagrant acts in violation of both Constitutions and the laws enacted thereunder. It is clearly apparent from their testimony that they casually regard such acts as nothing more than the performance of their ordinary duties for which the City employs and pays them.

After discussing the *Wolf* and *Irvine* cases, Justice Traynor said,

> Pursuant to the suggestion of the United States Supreme Court [in *Irvine*], we have reconsidered the rule we have heretofore followed [as to exclusion] . . . [W]e have concluded . . . that evidence obtained in violation of the constitutional guarantees [should be] inadmissible. . . . We have been compelled to reach that conclusion because other remedies have completely failed to secure compliance with the constitutional provisions on the part of police officials with the attendant results that the courts under the old rule have been constantly required to participate in, and in effect condone, the lawless activities of law enforcement officers.

Reaction to the *Cahan* decision was sharp among many law-enforcement officers. Chief Parker condemned it bitterly. Assistant Attorney General Linn said it was "the Magna Carta of the criminal. In this electronic age, it is equivalent to a law disarming police officers, saying they cannot carry guns." District Attorney Roll of Los Angeles, however, praised the ruling, an action somewhat unexpected in light of his long record of authorizing microphone and wiretap installations by Russell Mason. Praise for the ruling came from most California newspapers, the local bar associations, and civil-liberties groups. Two years later, Attorney General Edmund Brown reviewed experience under the *Cahan* rule and declared that its "over-all effects" had been "excellent."

This was not to be the only major development in California stemming from the post-*Irvine* mood. In 1957, the California Senate Judiciary Committee held far-ranging hearings into wiretapping and bugging in the state. The extensiveness of police and private-detective taps was laid on the record, primarily through the reluctant testimony of law-enforcement officers and technicians they employed. (Russell Mason, for example, detailed his bugging services for dozens of state and local law-enforcement agencies throughout the state. He also provided an account of how he bugged auto salesrooms, department stores, and hotel lobbies for their owners, as well as placing a mike in a casket during a private investigation involving a leading California mortuary.)

On August 7, 1957, the California Supreme Court held that the suit brought by Civil Liberties Union Attorney A. L. Wirin for an injunction to stop Chief Parker from using public funds to install dictographs could be maintained. The Court said that Parker's pleadings in the courts below in the injunction suit had indicated that he intended to continue authorizing such conduct, and he had not changed his position after the *Irvine* decision in 1954. They ruled that, unless there was a clear finding when the case went back to trial that Chief Parker was not authorizing and did not intend to authorize dictograph surveillance, Wirin should have his injunction granted.

(Some California police officials take the view that it was the Los Angeles police department that brought all the "Cahan trouble" on state law-enforcers. Every case in the California appellate courts between 1940 and the *Irvine* decision that had involved wiretapping and bugging had come from Los Angeles. Other police departments in California had used eaves-dropping information for leads to regular evidence and had not presented testimony on eavesdropped conversations to the courts.)

Following the *Wirin* v. *Parker* decision, Chief Parker stipulated that he would authorize no more dictographs. However, from 1957 to the present, he has criticized the *Cahan* and *Parker* rulings, claiming that the rise in the crime rate in Los Angeles and California is directly traceable to these handcuffs placed on law enforcement. Supporters of the *Cahan* ruling have challenged his figures and the battle about causation is still being waged.

All attempts by Chief Parker and the California Peace Officers Association to have the state legislature change the *Cahan* rule or authorize wiretapping and eavesdropping by court order have thus far failed. In California's new atmosphere, several private detectives have been tried and convicted of unlawful tapping. In February 1961, Russell Mason, who had said that after the *Cahan* decision his work had shifted so that he spent only one-quarter of his time eavesdropping for the police, was arrested and held for trial in Los Angeles on charges of illegal telephone-tapping for a private client in a divorce case.

The Supreme Court Also Reconsiders

The reverberations from the *Irvine* case reached the United States Supreme Court in June 1961. In *Mapp* v. *Ohio,* a 5-to-4 majority overruled the *Wolf* precedent and announced a new constitutional rule of due process: "all evidence obtained by [unreasonable] searches and seizures in violation of the Constitution is . . . inadmissible in a state court." The "swing" Justice in the *Mapp* case and the man who wrote for the Court was Tom C. Clark.

Dolly Mapp had been arrested in 1957 by Cleveland police officers and had been convicted under an Ohio statute that punished the knowing possession of obscene books or pictures. The police had gone to Miss Mapp's home (the second floor of a two-family house) on information from an informant that someone in connection with a bombing was there and also that large amounts of "policy paraphernalia" were in her residence. When the police arrived, they knocked and asked for admittance. Miss Mapp asked whether they had a search warrant, and when they said they did not, she refused them entry. The officers called their headquarters and waited outside the house. Three hours later, additional officers arrived, pried off the outside screen door, attempted to "kick in the door," and finally broke a pane of glass to open the door from the inside. As Justice Clark described the next sequence of events:

> It appears that Miss Mapp was halfway down the stairs from the upper floor to the front door when the officers, in this highhanded manner, broke into the hall. She demanded to see the search warrant. A paper, claimed to be a warrant, was held up by one of the officers. She grabbed the "warrant" and placed it in her bosom. A struggle ensued in which the officers recovered the piece of paper and as a result of which they handcuffed appellant because she had been "belligerent." . . . Running roughshod over appellant, a policeman "grabbed" her, "twisted [her] hand," and she "yelled [and] pleaded with him" because "it was hurting."

Miss Mapp was then forced by the policemen to go upstairs to her bedroom where her room and furniture were searched. Then the entire second floor was searched, and, finally, the first floor and basement of the house. Partly in Miss Mapp's quarters and partly in the basement, the officers found several pictures and pamphlets which served as the key pieces of evidence in Miss Mapp's trial. (Miss Mapp and another witness testified these had been left by a boarder who had just gone to New York.) The police did not prove at the trial that any search warrant had even been issued by a judge and the Supreme Court thought it highly doubtful that one had been obtained. Miss Mapp received a one- to seven-year prison sentence.

Clark Reviews the Record

Justice Clark's discussion focused primarily on developments between the *Wolf* case in 1949 and the situation in 1961. He noted the California Supreme Court's switch to the exclusionary-evidence rule and their conclusion that other remedies had simply failed to protect privacy and secure police compliance. Now, the Supreme Court must "close the only courtroom door remaining open to evidence secured by official lawlessness in flagrant abuse" of the constitutional right to privacy. Clark noted that the Court did not hesitate to enforce the rights of free speech, free press, and a fair trial upon the states; the same standard, he said, should be applied to the right to privacy enunciated in *Wolf*. To protect the right to fair trial, the Supreme Court had excluded all coerced confessions from use in state courts, despite the accuracy of such confessions. Finally, Clark stated that ever since the case of *Boyd* v. *United States*, in 1886, the Supreme Court had noted a close connection between the Fourth Amendment's right to privacy and the Fifth Amendment's guarantee against self-incrimination; this relationship strengthened the argument for a rule of exclusion in both situations.

Clark's peroration reflected the passion that the illegal-search cases evoked from the Justices:

> The ignoble short cut to conviction left open to the States tends to destroy the entire system of constitutional restraints on which the liberties of the people rest. Because [the right of privacy] is enforceable in the same manner and to like effect as other basic rights secured by the Due Process Clause, we can no longer permit it to be revocable at the whim of any police officer who, in the name of law enforcement itself, chooses to suspend its enjoyment.

Black and Douglas Expand the Argument

Justice Black wrote a concurring opinion. Reflecting on the *Wolf*, *Rochin*, and *Irvine* cases, he reminded his readers that he and Douglas had never accepted the "shock-the-conscience" test used by the majority in those rulings. Speaking of *Irvine*, he commented that "the five opinions written by the Court in that case demonstrate the utter confusion and uncertainty that had been brought about by the *Wolf* and *Rochin* decisions. . . ." This confusion promised to end only now that the Court was installing a "precise, intelligible and more predictable constitutional doctrine. . . ." Assuming that this new doctrine rested on the complementary relation of the Fourth and Fifth Amendments, Black said he would change his previous position (that the Fourth Amendment did not require exclusion of evidence) and would support exclusion for all illegal search-and-seizure cases.

Justice Douglas' concurring opinion added a further reason for abandoning the *Wolf* rule. That doctrine had encouraged federal and state police to engage in "working arrangements" to obtain evidence illegally and use it in the state courts. Now this practice would stop.

Four Read the Record Differently

Four Justices dissented—John Marshall Harlan, Felix Frankfurter, Charles E. Whittaker, and Potter Stewart. Harlan, who had replaced Robert Jackson after the latter's death in 1954, wrote an opinion for himself, Frankfurter, and Whittaker that the late Justice Jackson would have warmly applauded. The Court, said Harlan, "has forgotten the sense of judicial self-restraint" and the respect for precedents that should always be its guides. Dolly Mapp's counsel had not cited or relied upon the issue of the *Wolf* case; there had not been a full discussion in the briefs or in oral argument on that issue. Yet the majority "reached out" to overturn the *Wolf* rule. Such conduct conflicts with the Court's principle that constitutional issues should not be decided upon unless unavoidably presented in a case. The *Mapp* appeal *had* presented a serious and important issue—the punishment of the "mere" knowing of possession of obscene materials. This, Harlan said, is what the Court should have ruled upon, and nothing else. The first thing wrong with the majority's opinion, therefore, was that it should not have been written in this case. (Counsel for Miss Mapp, when asked during oral argument whether he was asking the Court to overrule *Wolf*, replied that he was not—he had never heard of that case. Only one brief paragraph in the *amicus curiae* brief for the Ohio Civil Liberties Union and the American Civil Liberties Union had asked for reconsideration of *Wolf*. In oral argument, the Ohio Civil Liberties Union counsel did develop this point in response to direct and obvious interest from several of the Justices. Justice Clark noted in his majority opinion that proper objection to the search had been made in the Ohio courts and in the appeal papers to the Supreme Court of the United States. Justice Douglas said the "casual arrogance" of the police in this case made it a proper case for reconsidering the *Wolf* assumptions about police conduct.)

Turning to the merits of the *Wolf* rule, Harlan remarked: "The preservation of a proper balance between state and federal responsibility in the administration of criminal justice demands patience on the part of those who might like to see things move faster among the States in this respect." Each state had special problems of law enforcement, state-by-state experimentation was progressing well, and it was a mistake for the Supreme Court to "fetter" the states as it had done here. Harlan considered the analogy to coerced confessions misleading, since that doctrine rested not on disciplining the police but on the violation of the defendants' rights when states wrung admissions from them while they were being held in custody; the violation took place in court when the confession was admitted.

In counterpoint to Clark's peroration, Harlan wrote:

> I regret that I find so unwise in principle and so inexpedient in policy a decision motivated by the high purpose of increasing respect for constitutional rights. But in the last analysis I think this Court can increase respect for the Constitution only if it rigidly respects the limitations which the Constitution places upon it, and respects as well the principles inherent in its own processes. In the present case I think we exceed both and that our voice becomes only a voice of power, not reason.

Justice Stewart's separate dissenting opinion agreed with Harlan that the *Wolf* case should not have been reconsidered. Stewart did not state his views on the merits of requiring exclusion. He did state, however, that the Ohio obscene-materials statute was a violation of freedom of thought and expression, and he would have reversed Dolly Mapp's conviction on that ground.

And the Friendly Restaurateur?

What about Patrick Irvine? All too often, treatments of constitutional-law cases trace the doctrinal developments and leave readers completely in the dark as to the fate of the litigants. This practice is particularly misleading because attention to the fate of criminal defendants shows that more than a few times the public interest stimulated by an unsuccessful appeal produces pressures that lead the government to suspend a deportation, reinstate an employee, or fail to press a contempt prosecution.

After the Supreme Court affirmed his conviction in 1954, Irvine asked Judge Pierson for a rehearing on probation. He filed a statement saying that the condemnation of the police tactics in his case should lead the court to deal lightly with him, and he promised to "plow a straight furrow" in the future. The probation officer was unimpressed and recommended that his original sentence be confirmed. Judge Pierson felt differently, however, and he considerably reduced the sentence. In place of one year in county jail, Irvine was ordered to serve sixteen days in jail, two days a week for eight weeks. He was allowed to pay his fine over thirty-six months rather than ninety days. For three years, he gave full-time attention to the Red Onion Café, plowing his "straight furrow." On May 3, 1957, his three-year period of probation was ended. Having fulfilled all the parts of his sentence and probation, Irvine applied to the court again. California law permits a defendant who shows proof of rehabilitation to have his conviction wiped off the books officially. This is done as an encouragement to offenders to become law-abiding citizens. Irvine's probation record was examined in Superior Court and found to be satisfactory; his verdict of guilty was set aside, a plea of "not guilty" was officially entered, and the information was ordered to be "dismissed." On August 7, 1958, Patrick Irvine died. Whether or not his memory is warm in the hearts of Long Beach horse-lovers and gourmands, his case has become a permanent addition to the nation's constitutional literature.

Patrick Irvine and the American Judicial Process

The *Irvine* case and its aftermath provide the raw material for a variety of observations about the operations of the judiciary in our political system.

The Costs of Constitutional Justice

First, *Irvine* illustrates the American judicial process in its textbook splendor. The Supreme Court of the nation, the Appellate Courts of California, the United States Attorney General—all became deeply involved

Mounting Public Anxiety over Wiretapping in the Middle 1950's:

1. Newspaper cartoonists viewed wiretapping with alarm.

"Hello, Dear, and All You Boys on the Wire Taps"

from *The Herblock Book* (Beacon Press, 1952)

Burke in the Chicago *Sun-Times*

Hodgins, Associated Press Cartoons, in the Miami *News*

"IT'S FOR YOU"

Mauldin in the New York *Star*

2. Magazines as diverse as the *Reporter,* the *Nation,* and *Collier's* surveyed the national party line.

The Wiretappers

WILLIAM S. FAIRFIELD and CHARLES CLIFT

Higgins in the *Reporter*

Hugger Mugger in the 57th St. Galleries
by Walter Goodman

from the *Nation*

3. Even religious groups such as Billy Graham's organization deplored the immorality of wiretapping.

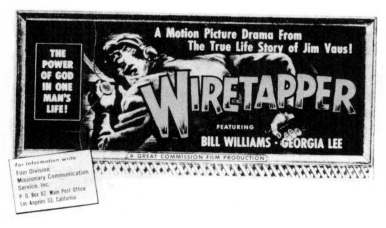

over the manner in which a petty bookmaker was caught and tried. Moreover, justice had come cheaply. It cost Irvine about $2,500 to carry his case from Superior Court in Long Beach to the courtroom in Washington, D.C., which is a lot of legal attention for the money. Such economy was possible because the record did not have to be printed, because Irvine's counsel fees were decidedly modest, and because he had no witnesses to pay or expensive exhibits to prepare at his trial. Other defendants in criminal cases, such as Frank Costello, have spent $50,000 to travel the same route as Irvine. Indicted political groups, such as the Communist party's national leadership, have spent more than $100,000 in their trials. In criminal cases, defendants without funds are entitled to have counsel appointed for them in federal courts according to the guarantees of the Sixth Amendment; and in 1963 the Supreme Court held that failure to provide counsel for a defendant accused of a crime in the state courts was a violation of the Sixth Amendment through the due-process clause of the Fourteenth.

When large corporations are defendants in antitrust cases brought by the government, costs are usually gigantic. Wall Street legal estimates are that Du Pont has spent $20 million in the past decade contesting Justice Department efforts to force Du Pont to dispose of its stock interest in General Motors. Even cases that do not reach the Appellate Courts can be enormously expensive. In February 1960, the federal District Court in Tulsa, Oklahoma, dismissed a federal antitrust suit against twenty-nine oil companies. The courtroom was crowded—with seventy-five defense lawyers. Senior counsel drew $1,000 a day and junior associates from $500 to $750. To keep themselves busy, some of the junior counsel calculated that the trial alone had cost the oil companies $50 a minute. Total costs were estimated at between $2 million and $3 million. The district judge lectured the government stiffly for bringing an unwarranted case. The oil companies, although pleased with their "vindication," could not deposit that lecture in their checking accounts.

When individuals or groups are not prosecuted but choose to bring test cases to vindicate what they consider "their rights," justice can be costly. When Joseph Burstyn challenged the denial of a license by New York to a movie he was distributing, the case that we know as *Burstyn* v. *Wilson* (1952) cost him about $55,000. The National Association for the Advancement of Colored People estimates that it cost "well over $200,000" to get to the Supreme Court in the famous school segregation case *Brown* v. *Board of Education* (1954). Today, the average cost of Supreme Court cases testing Southern compliance with the *Brown* ruling runs "between $50,000 and $100,000." These expenses are substantial because of the lengthy trial court record in desegregation cases. If regular lawyers' fees were included, the figures per case would be higher, but counsel from the NAACP's national office are paid annual salaries and local cooperating lawyers are paid only from $25 to $50 a day while the trials are in progress.

Joseph Burstyn was able to deduct his legal expenses from his income taxes as a business cost required to defend his property rights. Patrick Irvine could not deduct his $2,500, just as the average citizen cannot deduct the cost of fines for speeding or littering the streets.

Some organizations active in bringing constitutional test cases have perfected techniques of cheap appeal. If the trial records can be kept very slim—which means that constitutional argument instead of extensive factual testimony is presented in the lower court—then the route to the Supreme Court is not prohibitively expensive. The American Civil Liberties Union's general counsel budgets "$1,500–$2,500" for the average case that the ACLU sets up from Trial Court to Supreme Court.

The government has costs too, sometimes matching or exceeding those of its adversaries in constitutional cases. The giant antitrust suits against Du Pont, the United Shoe Machinery Corporation, and the electric companies convicted of price-rigging in 1961 entailed vast outlays by the government in investigative costs and the time of government economists, accountants, and lawyers. Adding to the expense was the preparation of exhibits and the regular legal printing costs (whether done by private printers, as for U.S. attorney's offices, or by the Government Printing Office for government presentations before the Supreme Court). Of course, the government also collects money as a result of some of its litigation—fines, penalties, taxes contested or unpaid, and moneys improperly charged the government by persons contracting with it. In Patrick Irvine's case, the state of California had the cost of the time of its deputy district attorney, assistant attorney general, and deputy attorney general in trying the case, preparing briefs, and arguing appeals. Since neither California nor the federal government keeps separate case records of their costs in each item of litigation, figures are not available as they are for private parties.

Liberty, Due Process, and Judicial Discretion

Second, *Irvine* presented the Supreme Court with a problem of "federalism"—the application of federal constitutional standards to the police practices and courtroom procedures of the states. *Irvine* typifies the "Fourteenth Amendment due-process" cases, such as those involving the right to have counsel, protection against the third degree and coerced confessions, and freedom from double jeopardy. Procedural due process is an area that the public regards as in the special care of judges, especially in cases of minor criminal offenders like Patrick Irvine and Dolly Mapp. When the courts issue rulings affecting labor-management relations, or adjusting the boundaries between church and state, or altering the power balance between President and Congress, there is usually much more public debate over the judiciary's qualifications for deciding these questions of "economics" or "politics."

Even in the procedural area, there is some ambivalence in public attitudes toward judicial assertiveness. Public belief in fair procedure may sometimes be subordinated to a desire to punish certain types of offenders—Communists or rapists or airplane dynamiters; the public may then disagree with judges who void convictions of these public enemies because certain procedural guarantees have not been upheld. Supporters of civil liberties then hasten to defend full constitutional procedures for everyone accused of crime, and a meaningful debate will be under way over key procedural rules, as with the boundaries of the privilege against self-incrimination or reasonable search.

There is, however, another kind of situation in which the judges use their broad discretion over fair procedure to strike disguised blows for liberty. At times, majorities on our courts will view a political conviction or a censorship move as unwise and dangerous, but not so clearly violative of a constitutional limitation that the court's majority can properly declare the measure invalid. (Some liberal activist judges may urge doing so, but will be outvoted.) Within such cases, there will often be errors in the trial or in the administrative process—involving instructions of judges, comments by prosecutors, statements of witnesses, and adherence to the agency's own rules in administrative cases. The judges have broad discretion either to call these errors "harmless" or to brand them as so serious that a new trial is required. Because decisions of this kind will turn on the facts and circumstances in each specific case, the judges do not worry unduly about making "bad law" for the future by this tactic. Such reversals thus produce a two-to four-year delay and give the community a chance to regain its perspective and equilibrium, while avoiding a direct showdown between the judiciary and the political authorities, and leaving unimpaired the general constitutional authority of government officials to protect the public in "true" danger situations. Judges do not advertise their use of this technique, though it is at least as old as the medieval era when British courts used technical procedural rules to free defendants from the impossible harshness of the English criminal code. The United States Supreme Court put its finger on the scales of liberty in this manner in several "internal security" cases between 1954 and 1957 involving deportations, loyalty programs, and state investigations. When American courts are accused of using procedural technicalities, the judges are sure to reply with an icy stare of denial. This is part of the public ritual, designed to quiet the fears of the unsophisticated. Students of our judicial process should still appreciate this method as one of the major, though not overworked, weapons in the judicial arsenal.

The Varieties of Constitutional Experience

Third, as mentioned earlier in discussing the costs of constitutional cases, the *Irvine* case was a criminal action brought by the State, in which Irvine defended himself and, while doing so, made certain constitutional claims. This is only one type of constitutional format. In other major types, the federal or state governments may bring civil suits, as for tax arrears, or to condemn land, or to dissolve a trust. Interest groups such as the National Association of Manufacturers or Jehovah's Witnesses may sponsor cases or support individual plaintiffs who challenge legislation or administrative regulations. Private persons, in their roles as taxpayers or parents of school children or doctors facing penalties for disseminating birth-control information, may sue to have the government restrained from carrying out a law. Individuals and groups may sue one another and, in the course of the cases, raise basic constitutional issues. In these types of cases, many of the judicial ground rules will be quite different from those in the *Irvine* case. Burdens of proof and presumptions of innocence will shift, different canons of statutory construction may be applied by the courts, and the general willingness of the judges to overturn government action may rise and fall in significant degrees. In short, although *Irvine* reveals the basic mold of the judicial process, other types of cases will present contrasting patterns in their rise, progress, and resolution in the courts.

Courts and the Political Process

Fourth, *Irvine* illustrates that American public law is not made in solitary majesty from the white marble temple of the Justices but is usually fashioned in a continuous interacting process with the political agencies of government. In the cases that come to it, the Supreme Court legitimates some acts and invalidates others. Those measures invalidated are then reconsidered by the policy-makers. If the Court's basis for invalidation was a constitutional ground, the policy-makers may do one of several things. They may dutifully obey the Court, abandoning their previous lines of policy. They may defiantly repeat the challenged action and make the courts rule again, and again, and again; many Southern officials in segregation cases are content to adopt one subterfuge after another rather than comply with decisions they regard as politically and constitutionally "insufferable." Policy-makers may seek and sometimes secure a constitutional amendment to authorize their program. The Sixteenth Amendment, for instance, giving the United States power to tax incomes directly, was required to overcome a Supreme Court decision in 1898 that held the federal income-tax law to be unconstitutional. More commonly, policy-makers simply remodel their statutes or practices in order to accomplish some or all of the desired results while side-stepping the judicial objections. Usually, tests will be made in the courts to see whether the new measures are constitutional, or just what the limits of the Court's rule were, and the process begins again.

Where the Court's rulings in federal cases are not based on constitutional grounds but rest on statutory construction, the policy-makers are in a far stronger position. When Congress disagrees with the Supreme Court's reading of a statute, the Congressmen can simply rewrite or repeal the statute. This was done some fifty times by Congress in economic matters between 1944 and 1961, overturning about seventy-five Supreme Court rulings. The Court has always accepted these revisions as within Congressional power—what Congress says, Congress can un-say. Some Justices (especially those who had dissented from the judicial interpretation that Congress overruled) regard the revisions as a proper and democratic interaction between those who make and those who expound legislation. Other Justices, a bit offended by Congressional revision debates that condemn "judicial legislation," have felt that if Congress had spoken more clearly when it originally drafted the legislation, the Court would not have had to fill in the gaps in a way that the Congressmen later disapproved of.

In the *Irvine* chain of cases between 1954 and 1961, the Supreme Court performed in a perfect illustration of this judicial-political interaction. The majority made general guiding comments about the reasonableness of state police practices and the values of exclusion. The Court's "guides" were received, sifted, and evaluated by state law-enforcement officers, lawyers, executive officials, and the state courts and legislatures with varying results. However, with the Court's declaration in the *Mapp* case, the Justices took the issue "out of politics." A judicial floor was imposed and state experimentation with exclusion is no longer possible. If neither Supreme Court reversal nor constitutional amendment overturns the *Mapp* rule, policymakers might try to use Congress' power over the appellate jurisdiction of the Supreme Court to bar the Justices from hearing state search-and-seizure cases. This was the technique attempted by critics of the Supreme Court in 1958, when the Jenner bill sought (unsuccessfully) to withdraw appellate jurisdiction from the Justices in cases involving state antisubversion laws, state teacher loyalty programs, state requirements for admission to the bar, and several federal areas as well. Whether the Justices, if such measures were passed, would follow a single reconstruction-era precedent and acquiesce in such Congressional action is doubtful. The effect of cutting off Supreme Court review here would be to leave in force the definitions of due process reached by each of fifty state Supreme Courts, and that would place a severe strain on the self-restraint of the Supreme Court.

The basic fact to appreciate is that the "federalizing" doctrine of *Mapp* was not an isolated ruling. Ever since the 1920's, the Supreme Court has been laying down federal minimums for state justice, and this trend gathered powerful momentum by the 1960's, reflecting such factors as increased national knowledge and concern about local injustices in law-enforcement methods and trial practices. In 1963, the Supreme Court held that states must give indigent defendants a lawyer in all criminal cases, and that the federal courts could examine the validity of state convictions by *habeas corpus* proceedings even though the prisoner had no valid appeal under state procedures. In that same year, an 8-to-1 majority of the Supreme Court ruled that state police would be held to the same constitutional standards and limiting principles that the Court had set up for federal searches and arrests. This promised an even more detailed federal review of state police practices than had existed prior to that decision. The dissenter, Justice Harlan, warned that this ruling would put the states in a "constitutional strait-jacket," and he urged that the states be allowed to work out their own rules of practice and evidence, subject only to the minimums of constitutional fairness. While a majority of the Supreme Court would contend that such decisions do not mean an end to local autonomy and state power under our federal system, the fact is that these decisions—as well as others limiting the states in legislative districting, school prayers, literary censorship, and state legislative investigations—point toward an increasingly federal definition of constitutional rights in the United States of the 1960's.

Judicial "Activism" Versus Judicial "Self-Restraint"

Fifth, the *Irvine* case set off a lively debate among the Justices over the proper role for the national judiciary in due-process cases. The fight—to hear each group describe the other's position—was between "mechanistic" rules and "subjectivity." Political scientists often call the debate one of "judicial activism" versus "judicial self-restraint." Some commentaries suggest that the division is an all-inclusive split within the Supreme Court. Several facts might be noted about this characterization.

If we classify the politically sensitive litigation coming before the contemporary court, we find cases presenting issues of equality, property, liberty, and fair procedure. In the equality cases, such as those dealing with Negro civil rights, the Justices have usually been united in a policy of active intervention against state segregation laws. In property cases, such as challenges to the constitutionality of federal regulation of industry or state and federal welfare programs, the Court has been almost as united behind self-restraint, or nonintervention. A deep split is found then in only two of these areas: in fair procedure, as we saw in *Irvine-Mapp,* and in liberty cases, particularly in regard to government's power to set loyalty standards, censor literature and movies, or give aid to religious enterprises.

Another fact to note about the activism-restraint terminology is that, to be used properly, it should be taken as shorthand for a number of variables in judicial attitudes, rather than just the degree of intervention by courts: Judges divide into those who view rights enumerated in the Constitution as "absolutes" and those who see these rights as competing with others and therefore "relative" in each specific setting. The "absolutist" may be a liberal in his political philosophy, such as the first John Marshall Harlan or Hugo Black, or he may be a staunch conservative, such as Justices Stephen J. Field and George Sutherland. The same is true of the "relativist," with Justice Felix Frankfurter as a liberal exponent of this position and Chief Justice Charles Evans Hughes as a conservative. And there is also a division between those who see all rights in the Constitution as equivalent in value and those who see some (such as the First or Fifth Amendments) as "preferred" to others, commanding greater respect from political authorities, and thus requiring greater protection from the courts.

Still another thing to note about the activism-restraint terminology is that these two positions may not exhaust the meaningful positions actually held within the Court. A third major view, one which would be best illustrated by Justice Robert Jackson, could be called "selective intervention," or the "equilibrium" theory of judicial review. Here, the Justice does not adopt the full rigors of either activism or restraint but suggests that the central cases should be viewed pragmatically. The Court should adjust the conflicting claims of liberty and authority, state and nation, private and public sector, etc., to retain those "great balances" that the founding fathers struck on such questions and that our political system has continued. This leaves the question of intervention to be decided on the basis of the key imponderables—whether the court's ruling will command obedience in the community, whether the political process has become clogged or is in a moment of localized hysteria that can be overcome, and other considerations of a similar nature. This third position obviously gives the greatest discretion of all three to its exponents, and in the sense that the Justices' decisions are always unpredictable in the great cases, it makes them fluid and shifting figures within the Court, as Robert Jackson was.

National Standards and Local Option in Constitutional Law

Sixth, what about the merits of requiring or making optional the exclusionary-evidence rule? Do *Irvine* and its aftermath shed any light on that?

On the one hand, the experience of California in reconsidering its admissibility rule and adopting exclusion can be seen as a vindication of discretionary flexibility in the Jackson mode. Let the states alone to consider the problem, and you encourage concern for constitutional rights at the grass roots. The debate in the California courts and legislatures served to focus public attention on police conduct and civil-liberties violations. By 1961, seven formerly permissive states had shifted to the exclusionary rule. "Discretionary flexibility"—the sharp lecture but not the federal sanction— can be seen as successful here in helping the state governments to move toward reform by themselves, with a maximum effect on local police behavior, local public opinion, and the like.

On the other hand, is that enough? Between 1954 and 1961, violations of search-and-seizure rules were repeatedly carried on by the police in states admitting illegally obtained evidence. Whether their practices were worse, or only better reported, than those in states with exclusion is the key factual question. Clearly, no one on the Supreme Court when the *Mapp* case was decided had any conclusive figures on that issue. Conclusive figures probably do not exist and it is difficult to see how they could be gathered short of an enormous, multimillion-dollar research project in fifty states that would somehow be able to get "inside" the local police departments for accurate observation. When the facts are not available in constitutional cases, the area of ideological debate widens to fill the vacuum. At least in the twenty-six exclusionary-rule states, many exclusionary supporters would argue, defendants are not being convicted through such "unconstitutional evidence." And, they would continue, the move of additional states to exclusionary rules is proof that the public really cares about its constitutional right to privacy. Thus the Court should institute total exclusion in recognition that this is required by community feelings about ordered liberty in a free society. In an ironic sense, therefore, the very "success" of the *Irvine* doctrine can be turned into an argument for the *Mapp* majority.

"Mapping" the Future in Search-and-Seizure Cases

Seventh, the *Mapp* case produced a host of important developments for constitutional law and police practices in the middle 1960's. When the ruling was announced in 1961, law-enforcement spokesmen in New York, California, Ohio, and Pennsylvania led police forces in condemning the ruling as a "devasting" blow to crime control. A drive was launched to secure a constitutional amendment overturning the decision, but as of early 1964, this had gathered no momentum in either Congressional or public opinion.

For about a year after the decision was first announced, the press featured accounts of state prosecutions that had to be dismissed or dropped because key evidence had been secured illegally. This was especially true of crimes based on possession of contraband materials—weapons, narcotics, obscene materials, or gambling paraphernalia. In New York County, for example, gambling convictions dropped by more than 35 per cent between 1961 and 1962. However, police applications for search warrants also rose sharply in New York County, suggesting that the drop in convictions would only be temporary.

After 1962, the state court dockets began to fill up with questions testing the meaning and limits of the *Mapp* doctrine. Was the ruling retroactive, so that prisoners now in jail who were convicted by illegally seized evidence could win new trials? Was wiretap evidence now excluded from state courts? Could police officers search without warrants by claiming that they had received anonymous tips from heretofore reliable informers and that there was no time to get a warrant? Are "routine car stops" and "routine personal searches" in neighborhoods with high crime rates barred by the *Mapp* doctrine? The state courts from 1962 to 1964 produced varied and conflicting decisions on these issues, and it is clearly only a matter of time before the United States Supreme Court will provide definitive answers.

The "Court" Is Nine Men

Finally, the *Irvine* case and its aftermath illustrate the irreducible element of personality in the judicial process. The Supreme Court is not a collectivity, nor is there such a complete allegiance to its institutional prestige that the Justices will put aside their convictions on public-law issues. The Supreme Court, precisely described, is nine middle-aged to elderly lawyers; what five or more of them say is the highest constitutional law of the land, and a new Justice or a change of heart by an old Justice can change that law overnight.

The *Irvine* case demonstrates these points nicely. This was one of Chief Justice Earl Warren's first cases. He came to it with his judicial philosophy largely unformed. Between 1954 and 1961, Warren was to move from the position represented by his vote in *Irvine* (with Jackson, Reed, Minton, and Clark) to a firm alliance with liberal activists Black, Douglas, and William J. Brennan, Jr. If there is any vote that Warren cast in his first year that he has come to regret, it probably was his vote in *Irvine*. Jackson's suggestion that the Supreme Court could discharge its own duties with a referral to the Department of Justice would not satisfy the "mature" Chief Justice Earl Warren. Had Irvine's appeal reached the Court in 1955, or 1958, or 1961, the odds are heavy that Warren would have voted to reverse the conviction, and this would have swung the decision in Irvine's favor.

Then there is Justice Clark. In 1954, his vote could have led the Court to discard the 1949 *Wolf* rule and introduce the *Mapp* doctrine of 1961. Why did Clark choose to hold back? His vote determined other 5-to-4 rulings of the Court between 1949 and 1954, including some that overturned existing precedents. His written opinion, with its public confession of discomfort with the *Wolf* rule, does not provide any satisfactory answers. Perhaps twenty years from now, some letter or memorandum, or some recollection of a former law clerk, will indicate whether an incident around the conference table, an article or report on police problems and practices, or some assumption about the consequences of exclusionary rules led Clark to this curious fidelity to a wobbly precedent that four colleagues were prepared to bury. Furthermore, Clark's stand in the *Irvine-Mapp* cases is even more unusual in light of his general tendency to uphold police powers and to view the need for order with utmost sympathy. Clark's major pre-Court career had been as a prosecutor in the Department of Justice, and he was often chided by his critics for being the "cop on the Court." Thus Clark's votes with the liberal activists in the *Mapp* case against police misconduct and in "threat" to crime control indicates the highly personal and variable aspects of judicial voting behavior. Few Justices can be dipped in analytical formaldehyde and classified neatly by species, for they are constantly hopping off "their" page in the album.

Looking back at the *Irvine* case and its doctrinal aftermath, an observer from another political system might read the *Mapp* case and remark, "Well, that debate is over." It would be the mark of emerging sophistication in the student of American government (and a last tribute to Patrick Irvine's beloved profession) to respond at that point, "Would you care to bet on that?"

Table of Cases, in Order of Citation in the Text

Wolf v. *Colorado*, 338 U.S. 25 (1949).
Olmstead v. *United States*, 277 U.S. 438 (1928).
Goldman v. *United States*, 316 U.S. 114 (1942).
Nardone v. *United States*, 302 U.S. 379 (1937).
Nardone v. *United States*, 308 U.S. 338 (1939).
Schwartz v. *Texas*, 344 U.S. 199 (1952).
Weeks v. *United States*, 232 U.S. 383 (1914).
People v. *Mayen*, 188 Cal. 237 (1922).
Rochin v. *California*, 342 U.S. 165 (1952).
Kawakita v. *United States*, 343 U.S. 717 (1952).
United States v. *Kahriger*, 345 U.S. 22 (1953).
Irvine v. *California*, 347 U.S. 128 (1954).
Screws v. *United States*, 325 U.S. 91 (1945).
People v. *Cahan*, 44 Cal. 2d. 434 (1955).
Irvine v. *People*, 113 Cal. App. 2d. 460 (1952).
Wirin v. *Parker*, 48 Cal. 2d. 890 (1957).
Mapp v. *Ohio*, 367 U.S. 643 (1961).
Boyd v. *United States*, 116 U.S. 616 (1886).
Burstyn v. *Wilson*, 343 U.S. 495 (1952).
Brown v. *Board of Education*, 347 U.S. 483 (1954).

Sources

THE primary sources for *Irvine* v. *California* and its treatment here have been the transcript of proceedings in the Los Angeles Superior Court (deposited in the Library of the United States Supreme Court) and the petitions and briefs filed in the Supreme Court, copies of which are in the Court's library and are given to leading law schools. The copy I used is at the Columbia University Law Library. Court records from California were also consulted, such as the probation reports for Patrick Irvine and the records relating to his resentencing. Newspaper clipping files of the Los Angeles *Times*, San Francisco *Chronicle*, Los Angeles *Mirror-News*, and Sacramento *Bee* on wiretapping and eavesdropping in California were examined for the 1938–1961 period. Persons directly involved in the Irvine trial and appeals, notably Morris Lavine, A. H. McConnell, and Clarence Linn, aided with recollections and supporting materials. The law clerks to the Justices of the Supreme Court during the 1953 term were contacted, and several aided in dealing with oral argument and the mood within the Court. My own files on wiretapping and eavesdropping in the United States from the 1850's to the present were drawn upon for developments in other states and for editorial and public opinion. I am grateful to the Columbia University Council for Research in the Social Sciences for support in continuing research on invasions of privacy by technological devices.

The most useful printed and secondary sources have been *Report of the California Senate Judiciary Committee on the Interception of Messages by the Use of Electronic and Other Devices* (1957); the hearings and materials of the United States Senate Subcommittee on Constitutional Rights, on eavesdropping and wiretapping, published between 1958 and 1961; "State Police, Unconstitutionally Obtained Evidence and Section 242 of the Civil Rights Statute," 7 *Stanford L. Rev.* 76 (1954); and Dash, Schwartz, and Knowlton, *The Eavesdroppers* (New Brunswick, N.J.: Rutgers University Press, 1959). For the author's views on wiretapping, eavesdropping, and the judicial process, see Westin, "The Wire Tapping Problem: An Analysis and a Legislative Proposal," 52 *Col. L. Rev.* 165 (1952); "Wire-Tap: The House Approves," *New Republic,* June 20, 1955, p. 13; "Wiretapping: The Quiet Revolution," *Commentary,* April 1960, p. 333; Testimony of Alan F. Westin, May 18, 1961, "Wiretapping and Eavesdropping Legislation," Hearings, Subcommittee on Constitutional Rights of the Senate Committee on the Judiciary, Eighty-Seventh Congress, first session, (1961), pp. 195–245.

D 6
E 7
F 8
G 9
H 0
I 1
J 2